CW00866648

The Dichotomy of the Self

A History of Ideas about the
Nature of the Self

Farah N. Smiley

CONTENTS

Introduction

The Fox and the Hedgehog

---

*The fox knows many things, but
the hedgehog knows one big
thing. —Archilochus*

Inspired by a sentence he had heard from an
Oxford undergraduate in a common-room parlor
game in the 1930's, Isaiah Berlin turned the
phrase (originally Greek) into a great essay on
Tolstoy named *"The Fox and the Hedgehog."*
The phrase divided people into two groups -
foxes and hedgehogs. It has now passed into
culture as a way to classify those around us, and
to think of two basic orientations towards reality
itself.

The fox not only knows many things, but accepts
that he can only know many things, and that the
unity of reality must be ungraspable. The critical
feature of foxes is that they are reconciled to the
limits of what they know.

A hedgehog will not make peace with the world,
he is not reconciled. He cannot merely know
many things; he wants to know one big thing
that will explain all of reality to him. Foxes settle

for the limitations of what they know and can lead happy lives. Hedgehogs will not settle, and their lives may not be happy.

Each person has elements of both the fox and the hedgehog. We must choose whether to accept the incompleteness of our knowledge or to hold out for truth and certainty. Only a few refuse to come to terms with reality – they refuse to submit.

Here, I will explore the different forms of knowledge we have access to from the perspective of various hedgehogs. Therefore, I do so in the spirit of the fox.

I am not personally invested in any worldview, but I find many interpretations of our reality interesting. It is not only that I find them interesting for their own sake, of course, but that I find in these ideas a kernel of truth that can explain, to some extent, why things are the way they are.

While it is true that I have approached this subject in the spirit of the fox, I have not forgotten my deep-seated hedgehog instinct. And it is through that instinct that I realized that there is an underlying theme while studying these grand narratives about human nature.

The Unmasking Trend

In the last few centuries, an intellectual trend emerged – it has been called "The Unmasking Trend." Philosophers and novelists made attempts to uncover what was behind the appearances of individuals. That is, what are the hidden unconscious motivations that people have? Freud, like Nietzsche, saw behavior and action as manifestations of unconscious instincts and conflicts of instincts.

The German Idealists Kant and Hegel had believed that the mind has total control over its own thoughts, in addition to the actions which those thoughts intend. In response to the Idealists, other philosophers – especially Arthur Schopenhauer and Friedrich Nietzsche—developed a new conception of the mind.

They suggested that thoughts and actions were not always under a person's conscious control. Instead, they are manifestations of a person's will, instincts, and desires. Rather than being under conscious control and transparent, the will, instincts, and desires are unconscious and often inaccessible.

Therefore, thoughts and actions come from a place that is not "I" but an impersonal and undomesticated agency. And this agency is as alien to our conscious knowledge as the intentions and thoughts of other people.

Psychoanalysis belongs to this trend, which was called "the unmasking trend" – it was particularly dominant in the late 19th century. The psychoanalysts continued the project set forth by philosophers before them.

But the hiddenness of human intention was not a subject reserved for philosophers and psychologists. It became a central source of inspiration and insight to poets, playwriters, sociologists, and novelists. And today, it is impossible to understand human nature without trying to decipher unconscious motivations.

Much of this book is the attempt to uncover the history of this trend, following it all the way through to the modern world. And throughout, we will see how much of the social world can be explained by the insights gained from hundreds years of philosophical, artistic, and scientific investigations into the nature of the Self.

And through this journey, we will address some puzzling questions that continue to trouble the mind.

Why does each generation continue to repeat the same blunders of the previous generations? Why does good often come from evil, and evil from good? Why is irrationality the close cousin of hyper-rationality?

Why does aggression often come hand in hand with virtue? How is it possible for people to feel connected and disconnected at the same time? Why is there a difference between intention and action? How is it possible for people to surprise themselves? And how is it possible for people to deceive themselves?

What is a Dichotomy?

There is a simple answer to all these questions. And this is not answer I came up with, but one that was implied by the best ideas we have about human nature.

The answer: the individual does not exist as a unitary Self, but as a multiplicity of selves. Not only that, but we seem to exist in a dichotomous state, and more specifically, in various dichotomous states at the same time.

This answer contradicts our normal conception of the Self. How can you demand consistency from an individual that is divided? What does it mean to be an "individual" (individual means "cannot be divided") if you contain many divisions? Does free will exist, given this new understanding? If an individual is not free, then do they make autonomous choices? And if not, how can anyone be held accountable for their actions? Why should anyone take the blame? And why should anyone get any credit?

First, what is a "dichotomy"?

A "dichotomy" is a division into two mutually exclusive or contradictory groups or entities. But a dichotomy has another definition: a branching that is characterized by successive forking into two approximately equal divisions.

In the next part, we will begin our exploration of various dichotomies. Gradually, you will see the obvious pattern that I saw, and you will wonder why it exists. That is when things get interesting.

1
Dichotomies… Everywhere

A Dichotomy of Perspectives

A prolific dualist thinker at the turn of the 20th century and the originator of psychoanalysis. Sigmund Freud believed that the dichotomy of our instincts was between Eros and Thanatos. Before this realization, he thought our instincts were divided between the need for Self-preservation, and the need for survival.

Jung, his star pupil, thought that our dichotomies are numerous and more complex.

There is the dichotomy between the ego and the Self, the dichotomy between anima/animus (male/female psychology), and the dichotomy between the persona and the shadow. Many years later, Heinz Kohut posited that there is a dichotomy between practical success and finding meaning, and that we gravitate two poles: megalomania and feeling of inferiority. Kierkegaard, in Either/Or, wrote about the dichotomy of man as having to make a choice between a hedonistic. aesthetic way of life, and an ethical life which is based on commitment to God. St. Augustine drew an essential dichotomy between the absolute beyond (or the spirit) and the body or the flesh.

Ernest Becker, in The Denial of Death, posited that man found himself in an essential dichotomy, between being an animal and a God. Rene Girard, the literary theorist, and philosopher proposed that the individual's desire is derived from the other. The dichotomy here is that desire for any object (fame, prestige, money) is determined by a dual interaction between the subject and their model. The subject derives his personal desires from the desires of a model or mediator.

In the Western world, this obsession with dualism can be traced to Romanticism. Freud's ideas are filled with dualities, and metamorphoses, which are Romantic ideas. Jung's dualities would be incomprehensible without Schelling's dichotomies. Freud's ideas can only be understood after reading Goethe.

In fact, before any of these psychologists came up with their theories, philosophers were busy coming up with their own dichotomies about human nature. Hegel, for example, came up with the dichotomy between thesis and antithesis. Nietzsche wrote about the false dichotomy in *Beyond Good and Evil.* Descartes is well known for his dualism, when he proposed that it was between mind and body. Before him, Saint Thomas Aquinas wrote about the division between soul and body. Plato, at around 370 BC, wrote about the difference between the world of shadows and the world of forms. Aristotle thought that every physical object is a compound of matter and form. And before him, Lao Tzu, the Taoist philosopher, wrote about dualities in the *Tao Te Ching* in around 600 BC.

Not only have dichotomies been with us for a very long time, but they are also a right-brained way of thinking, which as McGilchrist explains in *The Master and his Emissary*, is one of two ways of interpreting the world. The left-brained, fact-based, systematic way of interpretation is like Enlightenment thinking, while the more intuitive, right-brained thinking, is akin to Romanticism.

Therefore, whenever we have attempted to understand our reality, we have been overtaken by different kinds of dualism, either the various kinds advanced by the Romantic line of thought, or the very dichotomy I just discussed, between the left brain and the right brain.

We may owe this attachment to duality partly to our lack of originality. Or it may be something more fundamental. For example, it is interesting how computers run on binary code. Information processing in the modern world and likely in the future exists as a dichotomous sequence of zeros and ones. Physicists describe the world as existing because of a relationship between matter and anti-matter.

The reason why I bring all these dualities up is to make the point that dualistic thinking is everywhere. It could be that we think dualistically precisely because our brains are divided into two parts that perceive the world differently.

McGilchrist makes a similar argument in *The Master and his Emissary,* where he explained how the formal structures of modern society gives priority to the left brain, and that this is a dangerous development. It is a development because the imbalance occurred gradually with time. The individual in Ancient Athens was much more balanced in his outlook on life. McGilchrist does not include the Eastern world in his book, so his argument only applies to Western society but in a world that is increasingly westernized, his ideas are relevant to most people, regardless of where they are geographically located.

The problem with a culture with a left-brain bias is that it becomes rigid and bureaucratic. The people residing in such a culture become more motivated by Self-interest than empathy.

A Psychiatrist himself, McGilchrist follows a long line of thinkers who have been tempted by a dichotomous framework. What makes McGilchrist's work interesting is that it offers a plausible explanation for how some dichotomies that had been proposed could have arisen. That is, it could explain why there have been stark divisions between opposing philosophical ideals, political ideologies, and even our scientific understanding of reality. Throughout this book, we will go through various debates in psychology, philosophy of mind, and epistemology that highlight the difference between two fundamentally different ways of seeing the world.

When you read about the history of psychological ideas, you can't help but feel that the ideas are very much a product of their time, but not in a trivial way. Usually, when people say that something is a product of its time, they mean that it belonged to a different period where people were into different trends and fashions. But it's a much deeper point to say that the very orientation of thought could lead to totally different ideas about human nature. For example, it is very clear to see that Jung was much more right-brained than Freud. The former thought about human beings in a more holistic way. Individuation, Jung's famous idea, is about a process that gradually unfolds during one's lifetime. The dichotomies he drew were meant to encourage a union between the various parts of the psyche, to achieve a sense of wholeness. Whereas Freud's goal was to achieve a reasonable and functional compromise between conflicting drives – a very realpolitik view of the psyche.

McGilchrist himself did not mention these but it would be consistent with his line of reasoning. In one part of the book, he compares Freud's model of drives to a hydraulic process (left-brained) whereas Jung's model of archetypes are like an electric or magnetic attraction (right-brained). Left-brain thinking is linear, it proceeds from one place to the next, while right-brain thinking is holistic, which is why any kind of 'field' is relevant.

By the way, in *The Discovery of the Unconscious*, Ellenberger details the similarities between Freud's ideas and hydraulics. There is no question Freud was deeply influenced by the physics of his time, which marked breakthroughs in hydraulics. Jung, on the other hand, seemed to be more influenced by magnetism. In the section about Romanticism, we will see how profoundly influenced Freud and Jung were by their environment, the technologies and the ideas that came before them. If there is one lesson from this book, it is this: Nothing emerges from a vacuum, neither ideas nor desires.

In an homage to the right brain, synthetic, holistic approach, which is largely ignored in the modern world, I would like to bring more context into the debates about the nature of the Self, by reviewing the slow evolution of the psychological enterprise, where and when ideas about the Self were generated, and how our modern concepts about the human nature are undoubtedly the products of our own time.

Dichotomy 1: The Master and His Emissary

The Wrong Master

I have briefly mentioned McGlichrist's work, but I should start from the beginning, the title. "The Master and His Emissary" is a parable that Friedrich Nietzsche told about a wise spiritual master who ruled a small but prosperous land. The master grew the land and appointed many emissaries, but one of them grew very confident, and began to see themselves as the master. The emissary used his position to advance his own wealth and influence. The emissary sensed that the Self-control and restraint that the master had were signs of weakness, so he usurped his master and created a tyranny. Inevitably, the once prosperous land was ruined.

McGilchrist compares the right and left hemispheres of the human brain to the master and the emissary. The right brain is the true master, and just like the emissary, is often viewed as weak by the left brain, which is conceited and believes itself to be far more capable than it is.

In terms of function, the right hemisphere is responsible for creative thought, while the left brain is responsible for analytical, linear thinking. Certain activities such as drawing and writing activate your right hemisphere, while others such as calculating and arguing activate your left hemisphere. It is possible to repress your unconscious thoughts if you abstain from using your right-hemisphere. If you only tend to urgent matters that require your conscious attention, and do not allow you unconscious to manifest itself in any form, then you are disrupting the natural psychic struggle from taking place.

McGilchrist explains our reality through this perspective of brain lateralization. He includes in his study neurology, mythology, art, science, literature, and psychology – to explain how the hemispheres of the brain are different, and how this explains why we experience contradictions in our own thinking, such as the mismatch between what we will and what we desire.

These differences between hemispheres not only explain the contradictions in our own minds, but they explain the differences between cultures, and most importantly, they tell us why Westernized civilization is headed towards social disintegration, ostracization, and mental illness. The left hemisphere is sequential, linear, compartmentalizes the world, logical, and analytic. The right hemisphere is holistic, complex, receptive. Each hemisphere knows things that the other hemisphere does not know. The corpus callosum creates cooperation between the hemispheres, by excluding the other at the right time. But if the other is constantly suppressed by the forces of culture, then the result is an imbalanced individual who can only make use of one way of thinking – a very short-sighted way.

Eastern culture is typically associated with a more right-brained bias than the West. In the Eastern philosophies, there is always a call to understand everything as a whole and form a comprehensive and intuitive synthesis or combination. Piaget, in his studies on children, also recognized in them a similar way of processing reality. They begin learning when trying to understand things holistically, not by dividing things into simpler parts, as is prevalent in the West. Such a method is useful for exploitation and for getting things done but isn't so useful for gaining understanding. In other words, you need to see the bigger picture for greater understanding.

> Accordingly, Western traditional military thought advocates a direct military approach with a stress on the use of armed forces.
>
> The Strategic Advantage: Sun Zi & Western Approaches to War, Cao Sehn

An intuitive example given by McGilchrist is to compare the two hemispheres to a technology business consisting of a salesperson and of an engineer. The salesperson forges new relationships and brings in clients, while the engineer builds systems and technologies. The salesperson thinks that the engineer is free loading of his talent, while the engineer thinks the same of the salesperson.

it is not just that the brain manifests itself in the world, the world also reshapes the brain. But the brain is not a monolithic entity, it is comprised of two vastly different interpreters of reality, and for this reason, one takes precedence over the other.

A Real Division?

As McGilchrist reminds us in his book, there has been a turn away from this dichotomy of thinking about the brain (left versus right) because at some point in the 1960's, scientists falsified old theories about the division of labor between the hemispheres. It was once believed that each hemisphere is responsible for important functions. For example, the right-hemisphere is responsible for emotion while the left-hemisphere is responsible for logical analysis. This was shown to be false. The brain works much more cooperatively. The two hemispheres together are responsible for all mental functions. But McGilchrist tells us that the problem won't go away, because "this organ which is all about making connections is profoundly divided. It's there inside all of us and it's gotten more divided over the course of human evolution. So, the ratio of the corpus callosum to the volume of the hemispheres has gotten smaller over evolution.

And the plot thickens when you realize that the main function of the corpus callosum is to inhibit the other hemisphere. So, something very important is going on by keeping things apart from another. Not only that, but the brain is also profoundly asymmetric, it's as though someone grabbed a hold of the brain and gave it a sharp twist, clockwise." But why? If we needed more space for the brain, then the brain should have grown symmetrically since the skull is symmetrical. There should be no reason for why the different hemispheres aren't perfectly symmetrical and yet they're not. McGilchrist takes this as a hint that something else is going on, that the hemispheres are differentiated in an important way. And it's not just humans, but animals too have divided brains. It is as if nature is set up in a way, where we need to simultaneously have two different ways of thinking to survive in it. We need the left-brain's ability to zoom in and focus on the details, but we also need the right-brain's ability to zoom out and see the big picture.

But it's not just philosophical speculation that McGilchrist uses to back up his argument, he cites neuroscientific studies that show what happens when one hemisphere is damaged. It has been found that it makes a difference which hemisphere is damaged. In other words, if the left hemisphere is damaged, there are certain consequences. And if the right hemisphere is damaged, there are other consequences that are different.

And the hemispheres even take on a kind of personality. The right hemisphere is more pessimistic about the Self, relatively speaking. But it is also more realistic about it. There is evidence that shows that depressed people are also more realistic. Even schizophrenics have more insight into their condition, to the degree that they have depressive symptoms. The suggestion is not that insight makes you depressed, but that being depressed gives you insight.

Insight into illness generally is dependent on the right hemisphere. People who have sustained damage to the right hemisphere tend to deny their illness.

There is a phenomenon called anosognosia, in which patients downplay the fact that they have lost control over half their body. A patient with a totally paralyzed left limb may refuse to accept that there is anything wrong. They will come up with the strangest explanations for why they cannot move it on request. This happens to some degree most cases after a stroke affects the left side of the body (involving damage to the right-hemisphere. The phenomenon of denial can be temporarily reversed by activated the affected right hemisphere.

And the denial of illness (anosognosia) can be induced by subjecting the right hemisphere to anesthesia.

Language

In a sense, language, which is a left-hemisphere invention, can only work by working with its own presuppositions. That is, any insight you can derive from language can only come from language itself. While the right hemisphere cannot articulate its insights because they are too complex and cannot formulate linear arguments with clear conclusions. It is open to new experiences and is thus the conduit to creativity. The right-hemisphere chooses what part of the world to take in, and the left-hemisphere merely chooses to either obey or disobey.

But because the right-hemisphere can lead to an unstable society, there has been a revolt by the left-brain, and now the emissary has become the master. Yet this emissary has proven to be a terrible master.

McGilchrist does not attack the left-brain or the function of rationality. On the contrary, rationality is vital for the health of any society. But he uses rationality in the proper way, by being critical of the rational mental faculty itself. He cites Pascal, who said that the end of rationality is to show that it is not sufficient. There is no point in using rationality in the world, if we cannot criticize our own tendencies, rational or otherwise.

Rationality is, in fact, undermined when it is not itself examined, and for this Self-criticism to take place, we must apply a new kind of reason, one that is more holistic and open minded, less materialistic, and narrow.

In the West, there has been a consistent movement towards a society that is more orderly and rational. Historically, we can think of the beginning of this period as the Enlightenment, when a fear of human intuition, emotion, and superstition led to a hyper-rational ethic that persists till this day.

Romanticism was a reaction to the Enlightenment, and philosophers such as Nietzsche and Heidegger have warned of this development. Nietzsche, a strong critique of rationalism, suggested that the materialistic worldview is not superior to the religious. Instead of the worship of God (antithetical to left hemispheric thinking), a superior being, man will worship inferior gods, that are of his own creation.

This includes political and economic systems. Both capitalism and communism are products of the left-hemisphere, they are modes of dividing the spoils of a lifeless society in the most rational way possible. In the West, it is the worship of consumerism that has prevailed. And therefore, there has been a dissipation of family structures, and a rise in individuality. This has led to mental illnesses such as schizophrenia and anorexia in urbanized areas in the west. In art, we can see the universality of right hemispheric thinking (Bach can be appreciated in areas as remote as Papa New Guinea).

The East and West differ with regards to interpreting reality. In the West, the emphasis is on taking a side. There is a winner and a loser, a correct argument and a false argument, and very little room for contradiction. Whereas in the East, it is the opposite. Children are taught to understand the world through its contradictions. That is, contradictions are a source of trouble in the West, but in the East, they are a source of illumination.

The conclusion of the book is that there is a powerful movement towards linearity, systems, organization, and separation, and unless there is a focused effort in examining where this momentum will lead, society is at risk of remaining hostage to the incompetent emissary, who knows exactly how to do things, but never what ought to be done.

Jung intuited this a long time ago. and he believed that mythology was another way of navigating the realm of the unconscious, since mythological ideas already existed there. Like McGilchrist, he thought that the unconscious should be deeply investigated and taken seriously, rather than cast aside as an inconvenience.

To make this point clear, it is important to understand the difference between Freud and Jung.

Freud believed that the unconscious was made up of the personal repressed thoughts and feelings. Jung disagreed, he believed that in addition to the thoughts that were personally repressed, the unconscious was made up of the thoughts of our ancestors – ideas that we have biologically inherited.

> "Whether primitive or not, mankind always stands on the brink of actions it performs itself but does not control. The whole world wants peace and the

whole world prepares for war, to
take but one example"

The Archetypes and the
Collective Unconscious, Carl
Jung

The things we say we believe are not
necessarily what we believe in practice. We may
tell ourselves that it is better to abstain from this
or that activity, only to see ourselves repeating
these same activities the next day. According to
Jung, this results from a conflict between your
conscious and unconscious Self. One is pulling
you in this direction, and the other is pulling you
in the opposite direction. This tug of war often
results in confusion, it is hard to understand why
your body seems to ignore your conscious
demands. Are you, after-all, not the owner of
your body?

That is why a certain kind of negotiation is
necessary. You cannot be a tyrant to yourSelf.
You must acknowledge that there is a part of
you that is outside your control, and outside your
awareness – as was intuited by the early
philosophers of the Unmasking Trend
(Nietzsche and Schopenhauer).

Dichotomy 2: System 1 Vs System 2

Other authors have written about dual thinking
and processing by the brain.

In *Thinking: Fast and Slow*, Kahneman alludes to the dichotomy between the fast, intuitive mind, and the slow, precise mind. He called them System 1 and System 2. His book is a careful analysis of the various ways our intuitive minds fool us, and how we can try to check our intuitions when necessary.

Gerd Gigerenzer wrote a series of books including *Gut Feelings* and *Risk Savvy*, where he argued the total opposite point, that it was in fact our left-brain that was getting us in trouble, and what we ought to do, was become more attuned to our intuitions. And that our fast intuitions were far more sophisticated in interpreting the complex reality around us. This is like the point that McGilchrist makes, which is not merely that a balance is necessary between the two sides, but that we need to swap put the emissary back in their right place.

Dichotomy 3: Diffused-Focused

In her book *A Mind For Numbers*, Oakley presents dichotomous ways of solving a problem, the systematic, linear way and the holistic, non-linear way. One is good for literal applications, the other is good for creative, out-of-the-box solutions. If you are asked to come up with a solution to a problem, you need to know which way of thinking is more suitable. For familiar problems, the ideal thing to do is to follow a systematic pattern of sequential thinking. This method is known as focused thinking. But if you are required to think of a creative solution, to think laterally, or in a novel way, then the better way of thinking is to stop focusing, and to allow your unconscious to make the appropriate non-obvious connections. This method is known as diffused thinking. This is almost identical to McGilchrist's right-brain vs left-brain dichotomy.

2

THE DICHOTOMIES OF PSYCHOLOGY

Dichotomy 4: Order vs Chaos

Taoism emphasized the dichotomy of chaos and order. The psychologist Jordan Peterson applied this idea to politics, where there are ultimately two dangers: totalitarianism and nihilism. Both are extremes of human behavior.

Totalitarianism is the result of too powerful a need for order, and nihilism results from too weak a need for order.

While both are undesirable, it is hard to agree which one is worse. In fact, this disagreement, over which one is worse, underpins almost every debate between conservatives and liberals. Peterson is viewed as conservative by most people, likely because his greatest fear is nihilism. Whereas the more liberal Sam Harris, another popular philosopher, has the opposite fear: totalitarianism.

Why is immigration bad to conservatives? Because more immigrants implies that there is more change and disorder (closer to nihilism). But for Liberals, it is the opposite. More immigrants mean more change, more disruption, more innovation. Therefore, immigration is desirable.

As Gustave Le Bon intuited, the conservative mindset cannot handle gradual evolution, contrary to what our intuition tells us. The most conservative people are addicted to the most violent revolutions. They don't like gradual change. It makes them uncomfortable.

It is precisely because they are conservative that it is hard for them to adapt to slow changes in the environment. The liberal is the opposite. They are comfortable with slow change, and with the environment constantly shifting. Changes in gender roles, gender norms, gender rights, ideas about nationalism, scientific knowledge, traditions, and religious beliefs are greeted by progressives and resisted by conservatives.

The incredible thing about this dichotomy between people is that it must exist. It cannot be otherwise. Without conservatives, the basic structures would collapse. The safe territory, whether that is culture, beliefs, knowledge, habits – is preserved, which keeps things from devolving into total chaos. Without repetition, and retention of occupied space whether physical or mental, predicting the future will be much harder. And if you can't plan, because of so many constantly changing variables, then you exist in a constant state of flux. An unstable and unlivable situation. On the other hand, if you remain too much in a state of order, if everything is predictable and known, then there is nothing new, there is no innovation, change, or progress.

But it is not merely that different people exist in this kind of dichotomy. Each person exists somewhere along the spectrum of extreme order and extreme chaos.

The problem is that extremists think that their side is always right and the other is always wrong, or that one is always ethical and the other is always unethical. Traditional media channels follow this narrative, and that is why they have lost public trust. They have followed this narrative, partly because algorithms reward hyperbolic, divisive, polarizing content and partly because it's a smart marketing decision.

The worse space to occupy in marketing is somewhere in the middle, neither here nor there, neither hot nor cold. Lukewarm content is also the most easily avoidable content.

But people aren't stupid. They can recognize bias when they see it, and many have turned their backs on traditional media. Of course, this creates a whole new set of problems.

Now, let's go back to social media, which I will discuss in more depth later. When people are pushed to extremes, they cannot think clearly.

To occupy a balanced state, a middle way, between these various polarities is an art form that is a very difficult thing to do.,

The *I Ching,* one of the oldest Chinese classics, preached the middle way, between the practical and the ethical. But finding the middle way in life is never straightforward. Often, you will need to make a choice between the ethical and the practical. The *I Ching* says that if a choice had to be made, then it must be the ethical one. Nietzsche, for one, would take the opposite position (practicality) – since he thinks objective ethics is merely an illusion.

But if we set aside the Nietzschean view, and we consider the ethical side of social media, what can we deduce? Does social media connect people, or does it disconnect them? Are the creators of these platforms making ethical or practical decisions?

It isn't easy to answer these questions. While it is true that many people have been harmed by social media, there are others who depend on it for the survival of their business. While it is true that social media disconnects people from everyday reality, it also helps connect them with relatives and friends who live continents apart.

But this is only one way of thinking about it. It is a top-down macro perspective. What about the bottom-up micro perspective? How does the individual experience social media?

Of course, the answer varies from one person to the next, but generally, the individual on social media exists in a paradoxical state. They are hyper-connected, and yet disconnected. They are hyper-connected to the present moment, and to like-minded people from all over the world, but they are disconnected from the past, the people in their real lives, and from those who don't share their views.

There is a healthy amount of disconnection that each person must experience. I mean "disconnection" in the sense that they must remove themselves from their environment. At the same time, it is necessary to integrate into groups. Being social animals and all that, we will harm ourselves if we spend too much time alone. Hence the use of "solitary confinement" as a harsh punishment in prisons.

But the problem is when you are pushed to any extreme, you will suffer for it. Too much isolation breeds insanity. Too much company breeds unthinking conformity. Both forms of pathology. If there is a piece of wisdom that one can borrow from Taoism, and distill it into a soundbite, it would be "everything in moderation."

The novel thing about the internet (especially social media) is that it redefined what it means to be connected or disconnected. Is the individual considered alone or in company when chatting with others in the virtual world?

Usually, it is good to occupy the Taoist middle ground between connection and disconnection, but what does this even mean in a world where the lines are continually getting blurred?

Are headsets and VR technology, would loneliness merely be a relic of the old physical world we left behind?

Both online and offline, there is a danger with too much social connection. When you spend so much time with people, you totally lose your sense of individuality and critical thinking. But context is very important. When I say, "usually", I mean it.

In the East, meditation is good because it gives people the chance to disconnect from the group - their personal lives are so filled with communal activities that they rarely get the chance to develop an independent thought. But that is not the case for all cultures. A person who is stranded on an island by themselves doesn't need meditation, they need a friend.

That is one fundamental problem with Western Buddhism, which has somehow become the vogue in industrialized capitalistic societies. Setting aside the oxymoron for now, it does not take into consideration the context of the individual's situation. Many people in the West have the opposite problem to communal societies – they exist too much in an independent state and are in dire need of more connection.

Social media offers this kind of individual a deal with the devil or a Faustian bargain – "in return for never being bored or disconnected from human contact ever again, you must spend all your free time here."

But there is a fundamental left-brain problem with the promise of social media. Not only is it a second-rate substitute for real human connection but advances in technology continue to mask this reality. If you think I am being overly sentimental or nostalgic, consider how you would experience social media if it was a physical rather than a virtual experience.

You wake up in the morning, and you decide that it's a good day to visit your friends. So, you get ready, and leave your home. As you walk down the street, a random person jumps in front of you and flashes a sign, "We Have Had Enough." They talk to you, but you don't listen and carry on. Another man in a raincoat stops you, this person, has a different sign, "George is evil." You stop for a moment, but then you keep going. For the rest of your walk, you are encountered by tens, if not hundreds of people, jumping in front of you, and holding a sign. They are not really talking to you as much as they are talking at you. Some have many signs, not just one.

By the time you have gotten to your friend's place, you have already wasted half the day, and you are too exhausted to talk to them.

Unless you are an exceptionally interesting person, most people will get bored of talking to you after a while. But social media introduced a new dimension to human experience, the opportunity to never be bored (or lonely). When you are walking down the street, you have no choice but to stop and listen to some people, and even engage with them out of common courtesy. But your mind is processing experiences at a regular speed. You have time to reflect on each encounter. You have time to get bored.

Usually, the experience of talking to many different people in a short space of time is exciting. If you are extroverted, then it's the best thing that can ever happen to you. But social media takes this ordinary and enjoyable human experience, which was typically experienced at a natural pace, and pushes it to its logical extreme. Again, there is this theme of pushing things to the limit. What happens?

Instead of encountering tens or hundreds of people over the span of a week, you encounter hundreds, or even thousands, in the span of a few hours or minutes. Every day. And instead of knowing who to avoid and who to talk to, you have near-infinite options.

This hyper social experience is Self-defeating. By being hyper-connected, you are disconnected. By never being lonely, you are totally isolated from yourSelf.

And ironically, by doing the opposite, by disconnecting, you become more human, and more capable of understanding things you may have missed in the spur of the moment. You may reflect on events that have passed. It is through boredom and idle time that you gain insight or come up with creative ideas. The right-brain can only work when it is allowed to.

Constant connection, like that of social media, blurs your vision, you become swept away by the torrents and mania of the crowd, incapable of any reflection. And you don't get the benefit from human connection either.

In short, with social media, you lose the ability to introspect and to connect. You get something like purgatory instead. You are neither totally disconnected, nor totally connected.

The French philosopher Jacques Ellul described the effect of technology on the individual in a succinct way (long before the invention of the internet): reflection is replaced by reflex. On social media, your state of introspection is replaced by the constant need to react to other people's comments and posts.

There is another disconnection which I mentioned before, and it is the disconnection from the past. The person who lives on social networks exists in a never-ending present moment – they are dissociated from history, tradition, and culture. And this disconnection creates a sense of alienation.

Because of this alienation, they become vulnerable to being swept by various strange ideas and confused ideals. They are at the mercy of social trends. The dissociated individual often joins fringe groups at the edge of society to curtail their sense of isolation.

Chapter 1: The Root of Psychological Ideas

A Historical Sense

Just like genes, ideas are retained over time, from one generation to the next. Richard Dawkins popularized the word "meme" in his book *The Selfish Gene.*

A meme is a collection of ideas. A successful meme is invariably copied and transferred to other parts of the population, where it competes with other memes for supremacy.

A good parallel can be found in Jared Diamond's *Guns, Germs, and Steel* where he discusses the life of a seed, that uses fruits to transport itself for great distances and by many animals.

A seed, like genes and memes, needs to spread to survive, and it does so by creating delicious looking fruit. Natural selection will filter out bad looking fruits (no one will regrow them) and over many years, the best-looking fruits will survive, continuing the spread of the seeds of these fruits.

Genes work in the same way, but their mechanisms work through people and animals rather than fruits.

And memes? They work exclusively through people since no other animal can speak or write.

We are thus carriers of ideas, and these ideas have lives of their own. They transcend time but can only survive if the human species survives.

They spread faster with the aid of technology – think of how the internet and social networks speed up the sharing of ideas. Before that, it was the fax, printing press, and telephone. And before that, it was… pigeons?

The danger with memes is that if we don't know their history, we take them for granted. Either we take for granted that they are false, or that they are true, without doing the work to find out.

The memes in this book are not dogmas you are compelled to believe in. They are ideas that we have believed in. They are usually conventions – the way things are at a certain time. But they often are not scrutinized, even by those who are considered intellectual leaders.

One modern psychological meme that go unchecked by many is "the need to be happy" – that is what positive psychologists are interested. They have boiled down the human experience to the need to be happy.

From a political perspective, this makes sense. How to create an efficient workforce? Make people happy.

But there is a hidden trade-off. Like most memes, the happiness meme comes with a price. And the price of chasing happiness is loss of meaning and introspection.

As McGilchrist said, through the neurological experiments that measured the effects of depression on insight – one often gains understanding when they are unhappy, not when they are ecstatic. The tyranny of happiness is precisely what Huxley warned about in *Brave New World.*

Other than happiness, there are other memes that have pervaded the human consciousness – the need for balance, inner peace, Self-love. But the problem, of course, is that these ideals conflict with our psychology. That is not to say that they are not desirable. Good health conflicts with our physiology, that doesn't mean we should ignore our health.

Many wise people in society tell us that goals such as happiness, balance, and inner peace are by-products rather than goals to be achieved. You cannot become happy because you want to, you can only become happy because of pursuing some other goal.

But even such an idea, as subtle and intelligent as it is, may not be true. For example, it is quite possible to fall in love with misery. A person may be so invested in this idea, that happiness ought not be a goal, that they make their lives miserable, thinking it is the prudent thing to do.

In short, we forget the trade-offs.

If you choose happiness as your ultimate goal, then you may live a hedonistic, shallow, and meaningless existence. If you choose meaning as your ultimate goal, as the psychologist Viktor Frankl recommended, you may embrace a life of privation, unhappiness, and misery.

Perhaps the best life is lived on the extremes. Perhaps it is one that is balanced. And perhaps, there is no pragmatic solution to human existence because each person's subjective experience is different. Meaning may be necessary during hard times, but without happiness, life loses its flavor. Perhaps there is no single insight that applies to all people at all times. And it merely human arrogance and conceit to think that there is.

Perhaps the best we can do is to avoid coming up with a general thesis for "what one ought to do" and understand instead "what people have done."

The true message has always been this. "Find your own path." But such an idea is bewildering to many. There is the often-cited example from the Monty Python movie "Life of Brian" where Brian, who is mistaken for the messiah, addresses his group of ardent followers from his balcony. In trying to help them realize their independence and absolve himself from leadership, he says to them, "You are all individuals" and they reply in unison "Yes, we are all individuals!"

Nietzsche is well-known as the anti-establishment philosopher. His message was always to never become a follower, neither to him nor anyone. But there are forums online with thousands of people who have done the total opposite. They treat Nietzsche like a prophet and his words like gospel that ought never to be misinterpreted.

The irony is clear to see. The whole concept of individuality falls flat on its face when you realize that the majority of people do not know how to, and do not even want to become individuals. And it may not be their fault.

My point here is that even the straightforward "be yourSelf" meme is fraught with problems. First of all, which "Self" are we talking about? Second, do people really want to be responsible for their actions? Third, what does it mean practically to be yourSelf in a society that constantly demands that you not be yourSelf?

The common trope about philosophy is that it is the "love of wisdom" – it may be that, but I think that philosophy is more accurately summed up as the "love of contradiction." It is Dionysian by nature. The best philosophers have always been the best destroyers. And instead of making progress on a practical level, they have always tried to make things harder, by forcing us to think again. Kierkegaard sums the idea up nicely.

> But inasmuch as with your limited capacities it would be impossible to make anything easier than it has become, you must, with the same humanitarian enthusiasm as the others, undertake to make something harder.
>
> – Soren Kierkegaard

But why make things difficult? They are already difficult. Why not aim for happiness? Because the alternative is to be a victim of simplistic memes, that we regurgitate to one another unthinkingly.

In one moment, the Stoic meme becomes dominant, in another, the Buddhist meme becomes dominant. Virality rules over reason. Such is the nature of memes.

All this to say that the only thing that we can truly retain from the past is never the ideas themselves but the spirit of the ideas. We should not learn from the Greeks how they pursued happiness or how they built their democracy, but rather the spirit in which they did so. To think for oneself, to pursue truth, and to question the dominant narratives of the day – those are values that will always be retained.

Everything else, including "individuality", "happiness", "inner peace", "meaning", and the rest, are contingent values. They work for some and not others. They work sometimes and not at other times. But it is always correct to pursue truth.

The thing with memes is that they are independent of human well-being. They don't exist for our benefit. They just exist. These memes, once they enter the mind, take control, and, in many cases, they drive the individual to harm themselves and society by chasing futile ideals. If philosophy can have one benefit, it is that we can use it to deconstruct memes.

The Origin of Memes

When trying to solve a problem, developers conduct an analysis to find the root cause, they do not focus on the symptoms. Medical doctors learn about your medical history before prescribing treatment. The individual, regarding his political and ideological convictions, or his biological impulses, should do the same.

Understanding where these impulses come from doesn't help us understand what we ought to do, but simply, why we do the things we do.

Take fear and anxiety. Your body is programmed to react to urgency by increasing your stress response. It might be unpleasant, but it's effective.

Fear is adaptive. Without fear, our ancestors would have been eaten by predators. The evolutionary psychologist would also interpret something like anxiety in the context of our ancestral environment.

Since predators were a part of daily reality, the feeling of anxiety and fear were very useful – they prevented people from being too complacent. Instead, they forged weapons, created better shelters. But in the modern environment, anxiety is mostly useless.

And here, we have a very interesting clash between a deep philosophical insight and the interpretations of evolutionary psychology.

To the psychologist, the feeling of anxiety is a psychic disturbance that disrupts the quality of life. Our goal as rational actors should be to find ways to eliminate anxiety, lest it impede on well-being.

But Kierkegaard interprets the same anxiety as a core feature of the human being. In fact, it is precisely what separates man from animals. Animals don't feel anxiety. They may feel afraid for a moment because a predator is approaching, but this feeling quickly subsides, and they go on living their lives anxiety-free.

That is not the case with humans, who always exist in a state of anxiety. And for Kierkegaard, this anxiety, if it is embraced, creates the potential of possibilities, the infinite, and ultimately, for him, a belief in God. The philosopher Slavoj Zizek makes a different point, but no less profound and relevant.

Evolutionary psychology accounts for man's inability to understand their own nature: we were not designed to. The cat was not built to solve differential equations and human beings were not built to understand their own nature. That is a very sensible answer that has been advanced by Steven Pinker.

But Zizek interjects and says that there is something insufficient in the evolutionary perspective because human beings always attempt the impossible regardless. It as if we are hardwired to attempt to do things that we are not built to do. And in fact, without this innate tendency, no great discoveries would have ever been made. The attempt to do the impossible ought to be an extraordinary waste of resources, and yet it is a trait that has clearly survived. And it doesn't seem to be the kind of trait that just happened to go along for the ride but is essential to human life.

Without anxiety, would entrepreneurs and scientists be able to innovate? Would philosophers be able to discover the deep questions of existence? Would artists and musicians exist?

It is always the willingness to act out of anxiety, to play around with the infinite, to attempt what is unsolvable, that has led us to discover great things. So, why is it that the psychological enterprise survives by making this anxiety go away? I cannot end the question here, because it would be silly to not mention that in some cases, anxiety can be crippling. It is not always a precursor to discovery or insight, sometimes anxiety is just a source of misery. In which case, psychological intervention is necessary.

But in many cases, there may be an important use for anxiety. The psychological dogma that has pervaded has emphasized the minimization of anxiety and the maximation of positive emotions. The tyranny of compulsory happiness and inner peace has so thoroughly pervaded the social consciousness, that it is rare to ever see anyone question it. Every psychological idea has tried to reduce human nature in some important way. In fact, that's what theories or models are, they are reductions of reality. In the physical world, it can be very useful to do that. Even if a theory is not 100 percent true, it can still be effective.

When it comes to humans, theories are still very useful because they can give a general impression about people. If you look at Google Trends, you can see measure the different interests of people across time in different regions of the world. That is, in a nutshell, what psychology can do. It can describe to you the realities that people generally face. And people extract from the general, a specific idea about the individual. Novels work in the opposite way. A great novelist will write about a highly individual experience, and from that, you can deduce ideas about the larger population.

But there is a deep limitation to theories about human nature that rely on general information. The most idiotic example of deducing from the general are measures of the happiness of populations. You have probably, at some point in your life, read that a Scandinavian country has the happiest citizens in the world. In the same lifetime, you have probably read that these countries have the highest suicide rates. What gives? If people are so happy, then why are they committing suicide?

Because statistics about general well-being are mostly useless. You cannot understand anything about human nature from mass surveys anymore than you can understand the mechanics of a car by measuring the average speed of cars on a highway.

While this may seem obvious to some, it isn't to most. In fact, the modern economy is built on the opposite assumption. To be more precise, the assumption is that general statistics is all that is needed to be able to effectively control human behavior.

Behaviorism is a theory that was created by Pavlov and then developed by Skinner. The underlying premise of behaviorism is that human beings can be conditioned to behave in any way you want them to by giving them well-timed rewards and punishments. The dark discovery of these scientists is that everything that goes on in the human mind in terms of thoughts and feelings have very limited impact on human behavior. People are motivated to act, not by their ideals or beliefs, but by well-timed rewards and punishments. Change the routine, change the person. All this is already very bleak. But it gets worse. The way online businesses make money is by taking this grand insight from behaviorism to its logical conclusion.

Not everyone who has an internet business does this. But the most successful internet business models are built on the darkest discoveries of psychology. So, it is not a huge surprise that these ideas have led to feelings of depression among teenagers and higher suicide rates. Many adults have also become addicted to these social platforms as a form of social validation.

Of course, none of this should be news to you. It is a well-known and talked about issue. The problem is that no one has any idea what to do about it. Either the government regulates these companies, or the companies regulate themselves, or people regulate themselves. Those are the three possible options.

Since the first two options are too complicated and out of reach, I will go with the third option, which is the most complicated, but within reach. If people are empowered with knowledge about who they are, and understand the psychological forces that influence their behavior, then they can make better decisions about how they should behave. In that sense, I am taking an unscientific, futile position and violating the main insight from behaviorism.

In terms of understanding the Self, we will visit various schools of thought. We will look at insights from various places. In the next part of the book, we will look at how the Self is divided against itself. We will briefly visit various philosophies and psychologies, not to synthesize everything together, but to appreciate both the diversity and similarity of the ideas human beings have developed about human nature.

And near the end of the book, we will question the questioner. What do we make of psychology? Has it given us answers to important questions? If so, what questions? Why are so many psychological findings unreliable? And why are there so many different schools of psychology?

The study of the mind should be the most important thing a human being can do in their lifetime. The mind is the apparatus that makes everything else possible, it is the source of all anguish and joy. But the field that is supposed to give us answers to questions about the mind is fraught with controversies. Psychology, and unfortunately, science, are in many cases more political than we like to believe.

The memes that dominate the world are not those that are the truest, but those that are the most well advocated for. In university, we are taught explicitly or implicitly that society is divided up in two parts – those who are engaged in messy politics and those who are devoted to truth-seeking. Of course, the truth seekers are the scientists. And those who are engaged in messy politics are the government bureaucrats and the CEO's. But the scientific enterprise is as political as it is interested in truth, it is motivated by power and profit just as much as "greedy" corporations are.

But still, there are insights to be found in psychology. Throughout this book, I will not take sides. I will not promote any psychologic memes as the final truth, but as interesting ideas to think about. And I will mention the critiques of these ideas, not to dismiss psychology as a discipline, but to understand how and where it has gone wrong. As I mentioned before, to gain any understanding at all of psychology as an enterprise, we need to go back to the beginning.

Mesmer Versus Gassner

The starting point of psychology comes from an unexpected place. *In The Discovery of the Unconscious*, Ellenberger traces the roots of dynamic psychiatry to exorcism and magnetism in the 1790's. In the below sections, we will borrow from Ellenberger concise but insightful descriptions of important historical developments. There is a later book called *Exorcism and Enlightenment* that goes into more detail on what happened during the Mesmer – Gassner dual.

The late 18th century is known as the Enlightenment, with thinkers like Hume, Diderot, and Voltaire marking a new way of thinking, away from superstition and mythology. But it was not as if people suddenly decided that they would discard their old beliefs and become secular skeptics. Europe was a place of intense debate between fundamentally different ways of seeing the world. A primary debate that took place, was whether spirits and demons existed.

There were many accounts of witch-hunting during that time, and usually, when people think of the literature from this era, they are usually referring to the countless books about strange ideas such these. The pervading ideas of the Enlightenment did a great deal to put an end to witch-hunting. France was the most affected by this rational awakening, while Germany had retained more from the past.

But something else was going on during that time. It was a duel between the Baroque and the Enlightenment, that culminated in a victory for the latter. But it was a very close fight, and when reviewing the historical records, it could have gone a different direction had the politics of the time been different.

The dual was between a German priest named Gassner who was a widely known exorcist. He was a maverick, an unconventional man who performed individual and mass exorcisms, and didn't stick to the script given to him by the Catholic authorities. He worked alone and he built quite a reputation for himself. The Protestants at the time took a liking to him, precisely because he was so irreverent to the Roman Catholic order. Hundreds of people with all kinds of problems were treated by him.

Thousands of others were on the waiting list. Since he worked alone, there was only so many people he could see. His patients either had mild or severe illnesses and were usually invalids. But the people who believed that his powers were real were diverse. Some were well respected, intelligent, and educated, but of course, there was also a lot of criticism thrown at him. For one thing, Gassner attributed all diseases to demonic possession, without exception. Eventually the authorities decided to put an end to his activities because of the social chaos that he caused.

There was another man, Mesmer, who emerged in that period, and who claimed that Gassner was curing people without knowing the real cause. It wasn't demons that Gassner was casting out, but he was unwittingly dealing with animal magnetism.

At just the moment that Gassner's fame was at its peak and was attracting the skeptical attentions of churchmen and enlightened rulers such as Emperor Joseph II and Elector Maximilian III Joseph of Bavaria, another healer came out of Austria to fascinate his own throngs of enthusiastic followers.

Exorcism and Enlightenment, H. C. Erik Midelfort

In 1774, Mesmer had discovered that he could manipulate strange forces in some of his patients. He called these forces magnetic. At first, he worked with real magnets, but then realized that he had the same effect on his patients by mere touch and concentration. He distinguished this type of magnetism from the one commonly found in nature by calling it "animal magnetism."

Mesmer became a celebrity in Vienna, he entertained the young Mozart and healed the rich and famous. But after his efforts failed to heal a Hungarian nobleman, Mesmer went back home to Germany.

In *The Discovery of the Unconscious*, Ellenberger sees this collision of religious and scientistic therapies as the birth of dynamic psychiatry. Mesmer accused Gassner of having unfounded superstitious beliefs. But the irony, of course, is that both men were appealing to invisible forces that could not be measured or verified by anyone but themselves. The reason that this moment marked the beginning of dynamic psychiatry is that it was the first instance that the paradigm of natural healing was took the place of healing through exorcisms.

The Enlightenment (1715-1789)

The history of the West is that of a few great cultural movements: The Renaissance, Baroque, Enlightenment, Romanticism. Each had their own philosophy, literature, art, and science, and a style of life – which all culminated in the formation of the ideal type of man.

And each movement had roots in one country before spreading to the rest of Europe: The Renaissance and Baroque in Italy, the Enlightenment in France, and Romanticism in Germany.

The Enlightenment has been defined as "the spiritual movement which led to the secularization of thought and State."

There is also Kant's definition:

Enlightenment is the leaving behind by man of his Self-caused minority. Minority is the impossibility of using one's own reason without the guidance of another. That minority is Self-caused when it is due not to the lack of reasoning power but to the lack of decision and courage to make use of it without the guidance of another. Sapere aude! Have the courage to make use of your own reason!

is thus the motto of the
Enlightenment.

The ideal man belonged to the aristocracy or the bourgeoisie, and his life was ruled by reason and social considerations. In France, he was represented by the sociable figure. And in England, he was public-minded and interested in economic problems.

The philosophy of the Enlightenment was practical and optimistic – it insisted that science must be applied for the benefit of mankind. Another feature was a deep concern for and faith in education.

In science, there was no authority. Analysis was applied in mathematics and in the study of the mind, politics, and society. Psychology tried to understand the basic elements of the mind: sensations and associations, and then to reconstruct, by the synthesis, the full fabric of the mind. Men like Rousseau tried to imagine the evolution of society, starting with different individuals who assimilated and agreed on a "social contract."

Until then science was possible thanks to the work of isolated scientists who corresponded with each other. The Enlightenment created a network of scientific societies, which published the findings of their activities.

The Enlightenment's enormous impact on medicine is not very well known. It inaugurated pediatrics, orthopedics, public hygiene, and prophylaxis (prevention against disease), among others, with its campaign for inoculation against smallpox. It influenced psychiatry in many ways, beginning with its laicization (the reduction of the secular authority).

But the Enlightenment wasn't just a scientific movement, it was a philosophic movement. The value of human happiness, the pursuit of knowledge through reason and senses, and ideals such as liberty, progress, toleration, fraternity, and separation of church and state

Romanticism (1770-1850)

Romanticism originated in Germany and was at its highest point between 1800 and 1830 and then declined but spread over other parts in Europe. Its impact had lasting effects on European cultural life in the 19th century. In the strictest sense, Romanticism applied to a few groups of philosophers, poets, and artists, but in its largest sense, it described a vast movement that was a general outlook on life.

Romanticism was a cultural reaction to the Enlightenment. Whereas the former advocated the values of reason and society, the latter was defined by the cult of the irrational and gave much importance to the individual.

Brunschwig correlated the rise of Romanticism to the changes in demography in Germany at the end of the 18th century. The urban population of Germany increased enormously, and a new generation of young bourgeoisie and intellectuals were without jobs. They faced a bleak present and adopted an irrational outlook – they turned to the remote past or remote future, and expected miracles to occur in religion, medicine, occupation, love, and everyday life.

Romanticism contained some essential features. The first was a deep feeling for nature, unlike the Enlightenment – which was interested in man. Romanticism looked upon nature with deep reverence and empathy and wished to discover man's true relationship with nature.

The second was a wish to see what was behind the visible nature, to understand the manifestations of the unconscious: dreams, mental illness, genius, and parapsychology.

Third was the feeling for becoming. The Enlightenment believed in eternal reason and its manifestation in progress, but Romanticism held that all beings came from seminal principles, which could be found in individuals, languages, and societies. Human life was not merely a long period of maturity that came after a shorter period of immaturity, but a "spontaneous process of unfolding, a series of metamorphoses" (what Jung would later call individuation).

Romanticism cared about specific nations, not just with society in general. And it was concerned with the subjective experience of the individual.

Romantic philosophy may seem strange to us, since it is so different from experimental science, but the concepts of Romanticism are very much part of our inherited cultural beliefs, and deeply embedded in the new dynamic psychiatry.

Jung's teachings about psychology are unintelligible if they are not connected to Schelling. Schelling's ideas of myths influenced modern dynamic psychiatry, including his view of mental illness as a nonspecific reaction of the living substance.

Freud's mental life was dominated by polarities (dualism of instincts, subject-object, pleasure-unpleasure, active-passive). Freud's proclivity to dualistic ideas was a Romantic way of thinking.

And the roots of "archetype", the murder of the primordial father, and "the Oedipal Complex", the anima and animus, are all ideas influenced by Romanticism.

Karl Marx (1818-1883)

Darwinism was a system of hypotheses to support the Theory of Evolution and was transformed by Darwin's followers into Social Darwinism, that gave a scientific rationalization to ruthless competition that powered the industrial, political, commercial, and military world during the end of the 19th century. Marxism was the opposite of Social Darwinism, it was a philosophical system from the beginning, and soon also became an economic theory, philosophy of history, political doctrine, and way of life. Karl Marx collaborated with his friend Friedrich Engels to create it.

Marxism and Darwinism share the idea of the progress of man, but their ideas diverge with regards to the nature of this process. Darwinism credits progress to the mechanical and deterministic result of biological phenomena, Marxism ascribes it a "dialectical" process which must be supplemented with man's effort.

Marxism's main philosophical source was Hegel, directly and through some of his disciples. Hegel's philosophy gave Marx the "dialectic method" – a way of analyzing seemingly contradictory concepts, and for discovering the common principle that would unite them in a higher synthesis, moving from a series of ideas to the absolute. Hegel used his method to create a powerful system of philosophical idealism, but Marx applied it to a mathematical philosophy.

Marx borrowed from Hegel another idea, that of "alienation," that man is estranged form himself. "Alienation" means that man has externalized a part of himself, which he then sees as an external truth. Some of Hegel's followers argued that man is alienated from himself because he created a God in his own image, projecting the best of his spirit outside of himself and adoring it as if it were a superior being. By ending this alienation, man would reconstruct the synthesis of his own being.

Marx modified this idea. Not only are religion and abstract philosophies forms of alienation, but there also exists social, political, and economic alienation. To Marx, man is alienated from himself because of class divisions. That is, because man belongs to a mechanistic part of a social class, he is in a condition which estranges him from his humanity.

Thus, a classless socialist society would eliminate alienation and all its consequences. Marx said that up until then, philosophy had tried to explain the world, but the true problem was in changing it. His philosophy is inseparable from action (revolutionary action).

Like Hegel, Marx thought that humans went through a dialectical process of evolution, but he saw the process differently. Marx's philosophy of history is based on the idea that history can be interpreted as class struggle, and the latter can be understood by the notion of an "ideological superstructure superimposed upon a social substructure."

The discovery of means of production changed the social structure - the division of classes and their relationships to each other. The ruling classes oppress the inferior ones and impose organizations and political systems. But the ruling class also creates an ideology, which includes morals, philosophy, and religion – the ideology reflects the social structure and a way to oppress the inferior classes, through the judiciary and other forms of government.

Therefore, one practical rule of Marxist analysis is: "Behind that which people say. behind that which they think of themselves, to discover what they are by analyzing what they do." The work of

Marx contains many analyses of what he calls "mystifications," that is those processes by which people deceive both themselves and others to their own advantage.

Marx thought that war was a way for the ruling class to "mystify" or deceive the lower classes, because the former wants to divert an impending revolution.

As described in *The Communist Manifesto* (1848), Marx and Engel did not think it was possible to shift power in a peaceful way.

In dynamic psychiatry, Adler's relationship to Marx is obvious, he was a supporter of socialism. In fact, he saw neurosis as a reflection of social relationships as internalized by the individual.

Adler gave a lecture "On the Psychology of Marxism". He looked at the ideas of Karl Marx and claimed "that his exposition has demonstrated that the theory of the class struggle is clearly in harmony with the results of our teachings of instincts". He also suggested that Marx and Freud agreed about religion: "Marx was the first to offer the suppressed classes the chance to free themselves of Christianity - by the new outlook that he gave them."

Marx and Freud are curiously similar. Both had rabbis among their ancestors, they belonged to a Jewish family circle that came under the influence of the Enlightenment, and the work of each theory is inextricably linked to practice. They both saw religion as an "illusion."

In fact, there are more comparisons to be made between the two, Ellenberger demonstrates.

Marx	Freud
Emphasis on the economic aspect of man.	Emphasis on the sexual part of man (libido theory).
A society's culture is a superstructure built on a substructure of class relationships and economic factors.	Conscious life is a superstructure built on the substructure of unconscious and conflicting forces.
The inferior classes are the victims of "mystifications," by which the ruling classes also deceive themselves (for example, war).	The individual believes himself to think and act freely, whereas his conscious thoughts and actions are determined by unconscious complexes (rationalization).

Man is "alienated" from himself because of the division of society into social classes, which bring forth class struggle.	This would be at the same time a "rationalization" and a "defense-mechanism." The neurotic individual is alienated from himself because of his inner conflicts.
In order to bring about the revolution, it is necessary to perform a "dialectic analysis", to bring awareness, and to provoke a ··revolutionary situation."	In order to cure the patient, the therapist must perform a "dynamic" analysis, bring the individual to awareness ("Where Id was must Ego be"), and provoke a transference neurosis to resolve it.
The goal is the establishment of a classless society where man will no	The goal is to have a healed person, without conflict, and fully

longer be alienated from himself.	aware of himself.

Ellenberger does not push this idea too far, yet it is undeniable that such similar patterns of thought exist between the two individuals. Marx applied his thinking to economic and social facts, while Freud applied his thinking the psychology of the individual.

The ideas of Darwin, Marx, and Freud created ripple effects that changed the world for decades and centuries to come. It is hard to imagine where modern science would be without Darwin, or how advertising and the modern economy that followed would be without Freud, or the state of politics today without Marx.

People tend to create a false dichotomy in their minds between events and ideas. It is as if there is a secluded world, away from the physical world, the academics occupy, and this world has nothing to do with their daily lives. But this is a lie.

As the philosopher Bertrand Russell intuited in *A History of Western Philosophy*, a more accurate way of framing history is to see as a dynamic interplay between ideas and events. That is, events create a cultural climate for certain ideas to manifest, and these ideas, in turn, lead to the unfolding of events.

Chapter 2: The Dichotomy of Nature and Nurture

A History of Instincts

The idea of instinctivism is that man is endowed with certain primitive drives such as the drive for aggression, or the drive for survival or procreation. And that these drives predict human behavior better than anything else. In other words, if you want to understand human motivation, then look no further than the instincts.

Two famous thinkers who studied human instincts were Freud and Lorenz. Both were heavily influenced by Darwin. But they were not the only ones to write on this subject. The American psychologist William James created a long list of instincts which were supposed to motivate many kinds of behavior. These include the James' instincts of imitation, rivalry, pugnacity, sympathy, fear, acquisitiveness, kleptomania, curiosity, play, cleanliness, modesty, jealousy, and others.

But after Darwin, the thinking on this topic totally shifted. We no longer think of human beings as being endowed with various mysterious instincts. The theory of evolution greatly narrows the discussion. From the beginning, all forms of life are interested primarily in two things, survival, and reproduction.

But to truly understand human nature, we must first look at the full picture. Are all of man's instincts explained by the basic desire to survive and replicate?

Charles Darwin (1809-1882)

After 1950, Romanticism and the Enlightenment began losing importance, although the latter could be credited for the emancipation of serfs in Russia and the U.S. These philosophies were replaced by the philosophy of the Industrial Revolution which emphasized free market capitalism, and this was congruent to Darwinian thought. Whereas Marxism provided the basis for the socialist parties that grew from the struggle of the proletariat.

The ancestor of man was as different to primitive savages today, as those savages are from civilized man. Darwin tried to give a biological explanation of the evolution of our ancestor towards the present human. He said that society was born out of the parental instinct, and the instinct of mutual help between animals of the same species. Language developed from cries of help. Morals came from these instincts and then reinforced by man's sensitivity to social opinion and then by reason and habit.

But in *The Descent of Man*, Darwin moved away from the struggle of existing, and gave importance to the role of sexual selection – that stronger men chose more attractive females, and these females preferred stronger males, the result being that these men would birth more offspring.

It is said that he was the first to spell out the theory of evolution, but this line of thought preceded Darwin. And Darwin proposed the theory of the struggle as a hypothesis. Today it is assumed that he proved it, thus the idea of the struggle for existence has always been a hypothesis. The Hobbesian "war of everyone against everyone" was thought to be a universal law that was discovered by Darwin, by Darwin's most enthusiastic followers.

It is true that Darwin's theory of evolution was widely accepted, but there are still doubts with regards to the true role played by the struggle for existence, and its effect on evolution – whether chance variations can result in new species (not only new races), and to the existence of most missing links.

Darwin's theory, had it remained in its original field, would not have gained so much fame. Its principles were extended to other sciences. Psychologists assumed that instincts and mental faculties have roots in natural selection, and that the evolution of human societies were reconstructed in similar ways. No branch of science was free from this kind of speculation.

Darwin was careful not to enter into the realm of philosophy, but his supporters thought that a philosophical system could be deduced from his ideas – especially the idea of evolution and progress.

The most important development of Dawinism was Social Darwinism, the universal application of "struggle for life," "survival of the fittest," and "elimination of the unfit" to the problems and realities of every society.

Militarists used this to argue for war. The pseudo-Darwinian philosophy persuaded the European elite of the biological necessity of war, and this contributed to the precipitation of World War. Hitler and many other politicians proclaimed the same Darwinian principles.

In short, as stated by Kropotkin. "There is no infamy in civilized society, or in the relations of the Whites toward the so-called lower races, or of the strong toward the weak which would not have found its excuse in this formula."

Alfred Adler reversed the principle of the "elimination of the unfit" in a systematic way. He showed that organic inferiorities were the impetus for biological compensation. This principle was a basic tenant of his psychological system. Inferiority, far from being a cause of failure, would be the best stimulate for victory and social struggle.

Freud's theory of the instincts is also connected to Darwin's ideas. Freud started by only considering the libido and later assumed the existence of a separate aggressive and destructive instinct, while Darwin followed the opposite path.

Paul Ree explained that the moral conscience issued from a legalized Dawinian struggle for life. Man has no right which he cannot defend. If someone wanted someone else's property, he could challenge the owner to a duel. The refusal to engage on the part of the owner, or his death in the duel, would result in the reallocation of the property.

Eventually, the law stopped tolerating this custom, and the frustrated acquisitive and aggressive drive of man became the root of remorse (conscience). This idea was developed by Nietzsche in *The Genealogy of Morals*, which lay the foundation for Freud's *Civilization and Its Discontents.*

Arthur Schopenhauer (1788-1860)

Dichotomy 5: Will and Representation

Known as the great pessimist of German philosophy, Schopenhauer's outlook on life was rather misunderstood. His views are not bleaker than the Darwinian idea that life is a ruthless struggle, and especially not bleaker than the Buddhist outlook. In fact, Schopenhauer's work preceded, and therefore, anticipated Darwin and the evolutionists.

Schopenhauer was aware of the scientific literature of his time which already contained the idea of evolution before Darwin. The latter's contribution was in building such a large body of evidence for it. Schopenhauer thought that life is an endless and uncompromising battle of all against all.

The history of philosophy is one of philosophers responding to each other. Schopenhauer was a critic of Hegel, but an admirer of Kant. To understand Schopenhauer, we must understand Kant's idea the way we perceive the world. Kant thought that there is a phenomenal world which is accessible through our senses and there are "things-in-themselves" which exist independently of our senses.

Since our experience of reality is logically confined by our sensations, we can never truly know the "world in itself." That is why scientists use microscopes to get a more accurate picture of what's going on - beyond what our eyes are telling us. The limitation of our senses was not a problem for Schopenhauer, who thought that reason could light the way for us towards the true reality. He called this thing-in-itself or true reality the "noumenon" and its primary feature was that it had to contain a unity and exist beyond space and time.

The counter-intuitive idea is that the world we have minimal access to, the noumenal world, is real, while the world that we have direct access to, and indeed, have the most experiences in, is an illusion. The representational world is constantly changing – everything in it either morphs into new forms, or else dies.

But the phenomenal world is not chaotic but operates according to "sufficient reason" or the laws of cause and effect. Even though we have projected this world through our minds, there is nonetheless predictability within it. It is a sensible world.

The laws of space and time are part of this conditional world and do not exist independently. Time, under this definition, does not exist absolutely. It only exists to observers, who must create representations along the space-time continuum.

Everything in space-time is relative. A moment in time is real insofar as it is related to moments before and after it. And in space, objects are real insofar as they are related to other objects. There are ideas here that are inspired by Greek philosophy such as Plato's concept of "forms" and Heraclitus' idea that things are in eternal flux and have no fixed reality. But Schopenhauer was also influenced by the East, both in his general outlook on the human condition, and in his ideas about the nature of reality. He borrows the Hindu concept of "Maya" which states that the world is an illusion, projection, or dream. And thus, it is open to misinterpretation by the observer.

Therefore, space, objects in space, and time itself are representations of the subjects that perceive or project them. Contrary to Hegel, who Schopenhauer is very dismissive of, the latter believed that history was not an objective account of events that occurred, or a process leading to a fixed goal, but merely a story told from the perspective of the subject. The past and future has as much basis in reality as a dream does.

The Will

Schopenhauer thought that the "will" is the core feature of the phenomenal world and is expressed in a variety of blind and purposeless strivings. This is the will to life. We usually think of "will" as consciously conceived. That is, there must be a person who "wills", but Schopenhauer gave the word a much broader definition – the "will" is a form of energy that is incessantly looking for an outlet.

This gives a justification not only for the strivings of humans, but of all forms of life and even non-life. As for the question of free will, Schopenhauer thought that each person cannot but act according to their own nature.

We feel that we only do what we *will*, but we cannot *"will"* anything else. In other words, our essence predetermines the things that we *will*. This means that we do not have free will, since we cannot change our character, motives, or essence. Most men, according to Schopenhauer, work tirelessly in accordance with the aim of this will. An idea that is one of the inspirations behind Freud's concept of subconscious urges. The Freudian ego is not unlike Schopenhauer's will.

But the defining feature of Schopenhauer's philosophy is that the will is not something to be revered or worshipped- as we will see later with Nietzsche, who had an exalted perspective on the will. Schopenhauer saw the will as a negative power that ought to be transcended, and like Buddha, the German philosopher thought that greater the intensity of the will, the more suffering it will cause. The reason is that all willing comes from emptiness, a feeling that something is lacking. While the wise person identifies with the formless and the true, seeing themselves as merely a temporary bodily expression of a timeless spiritual substance, the uneducated or wicked person totally embraces their body and will. This wicked person thinks that they are truly independent and everyone and everything else is not as important.

But the individual *will* is, of course, less important than the general will that is behind everything. Therefore, too strong an identification with the ego, or with oneself, is a precursor to a life of illusion. The person identified with their own *will* cannot see the grander vision of reality, which is integrated and uniform. Rather, this individual is only capable of seeing divisions and separations. They can only see phenomena as essentially different and opposed. In other words, the person who has separated their personal will from the global will of nature, has at the same time identified with the reality of the dichotomy that they are perceive. They really see things in nature that are opposed to each other as things in conflict, and not part of a complimentary whole. And ultimately, as mentioned before, this is a left-brained bias.

In contrast to those who see the world as separate to themselves, those who see a union with nature are more likely to find a path towards freedom, according to Schopenhauer. The idea here is that the Self, that we have constructed over time, is actually an illusion - it is not a "thing-in-itself." It is a projection, and its source is our own minds. In fact, there is a simple way to prove that it is a projection. Each person sees you differently. Your friend does not perceive you in the same way that your dog or brother or business partner does. And none of them perceive you the way you perceive yourSelf. In politics, there is a saying, "one man's terrorist is another man's freedom fighter." It may be a more profound statement than it seems.

When the individual understands that there is no "I", then they are free from the cycle of birth, old age, sickness, and death and imprisonment within time, space, and the laws of causality. The wise individual, according to Schopenhauer, sees good and bed, pleasure and pain, as mere phenomena that are different expressions of

Oneness. There was an obvious route towards this non-identification of "I" and it was through the monastic life since this allowed the person to reject sensual pleasures. But there is another way, and it is through the experience of nature or art.

The default mode of the mind is incessant analyzing and reasoning. But it is possible to give our whole minds to the present moment. When looking at a landscape, we can forget our individuality, our will, and exist as a pure subject, or as a pure mirror of the object. While this seems like a narcissistic and Selfish way of living, it is the opposite according to Schopenhauer, and of course, the Eastern religions. Once you no longer identify with the Self, with the "I", then you will have far more compassions for others and for nature.

Friedrich Nietzsche (1844-1900)

Nietzsche was a German philologist who has been credited with the rise of Nazism. The titles of his books, *The Anti-Christ* and *Beyond Good or Evil* are hardly good defenses against these accusations. To understand Nietzsche is key to understanding the emergence of psychoanalysis. But to understand Nietzsche, we must remember that he too was a product of his time.

Nietzsche was aware of Darwin's work and was influenced by Schopenhauer.

The Prophet of Human Psychology

Science has been described by Nietzsche as a disguised wish for death. That science is a "principal inimical to life and destructive. The will for truth could be a disguised wish for death." Since science affirms a world that is different from our own, it is therefore the negation of our world (the world of life).

Is science inimical to life? Does the Self aim towards death? Or are these the scribbles of a mad philosopher?

Interestingly, Freud spoke about the death drive, Thanatos, as the antithesis of the life drive, Eros. In fact, Freud, Adler, and Jung – the pioneers of psychoanalysis – are all heavily influenced by Nietzsche's ideas, so much so that their main contributions to psychology have clear Nietzschean roots. The idea that we are unconsciously moving civilization towards Self-destruction is well-founded, and before we dismiss Nietzsche as a renegade mad man, let us take a brief tour, and get a glimpse of how profound his influence was on the birth of psychoanalysis.

The superman idea by Nietzsche, that is, that "man is something that must be overcome" (Zarathustra's first message) has its equivalent in Adler's principle "to be human means to be stimulated by a feeling of inferiority which aims at being overcome." The idea that the one basic drive in man is the will to power is reflected in Adler's idea of man's basic striving toward superiority.

Nietzsche's works contain many examples of how the will to power manifests under many disguised forms. The main difference between Adler and Nietzsche is that Adler accepts the "community feeling" as a way for man to overcome himself while Nietzsche, a radical individualist, thought that the "herd instinct" was contemptible. But Nietzsche's idea that "the error about life is necessary to life" and that Self-deceit is necessary to the individual are similar to Adler's idea of the "guiding fiction" of the neurotic.'

Freud speaks of Nietzsche as a philosopher "whose guesses and intuitions often agree in the most astonishing way with the laborious findings of psychoanalysis."

Ellenberger, The Discovery of the Unconscious

This is not to say that Nietzsche was a wholly original thinker, many of his ideas can also be traced to different authors, but his insight into the human condition may have few parallels in the history of philosophy.

Carl Jung was fascinated by Nietzsche's philosophy, and he was very open about it, working on a series of unpublished lectures on Nietzsche's *Thus Spoke Zarathustra*. Many of Jung's idea are modified forms of Nietzsche's ideas, including his reflection on the problem of evil, the superior instincts in man, the unconscious, the dream, archetypes, the shadow, the persona, the old wise man, and other concepts. Jung thought that Zarathustra was Nietzsche's secondary personality that slowly developed in his unconscious until it suddenly erupted with an enormous amount of archetypal material.

And yet Nietzsche also warned about the death instinct, about the innate urge for destruction. And when we look around us, we cannot help but observe prosperity and technological progress and be thankful for the era we live in. But we should also consider the amount of destruction that scientific progress has heaped on the lives of millions of people and continues to do so, with nuclear war and biological war being real possibilities.

The irony, however, is that Nietzsche has such a profound influence on the discipline that was supposed to help people recover from mental sickness. Nietzsche himself was far from a psychologically healthy character and many of his ideas were amoral and mistaken, but some were provocative and honest. While Nietzsche may not have described how things ought to be, he did describe how they are – at least, how he thought they were.

Dichotomy 2: Herd Morality vs Master Morality

Based on Hegel's Master-slave dialectic, Nietzsche proposed that there are two fundamental types of morality: "master morality" and "slave morality."

Nietzsche thought that there is a natural hierarchy to mankind – a cosmic justice. The noble soul, or the master, does not look above them, but only forwards or down, because he knows that "he is on a height."

Yet religion, education, and culture suggest that we would be fulfilled by making ourselves smaller than others. This, to Nietzsche, was a well-veiled lie. The individual is deceived into priding themselves with mediocre qualities rather than having a strong spirit.

Master morality prized power and pride, while slave morality cherished qualities such as kindness and empathy. Master morality saw that good actions were those that were associated with noble men, while bad actions were associated with the rabble.

On the other hand, slave morality makes judgements on actions based on an independent moral standard, whether a religious one, such as that of Christianity, or a philosophical one, such as Kant's deontology.

Master Morality

People who were strong had a master morality. The idea of the British Utilitarian John Stuart Mill who saw that good behavior served the common good, while bad behavior harmed the common good, was criticized by Nietzsche.

He wrote that in the prehistoric state, "the value or non-value of an action was derived from its consequences"[1] but that ultimately "[t]here are no moral phenomena at all, only moral interpretations of phenomena."[2] For strong-willed men, the "good" is the noble, strong, and powerful, while the "bad" is the weak, cowardly, timid, and petty.

To say that there are no moral phenomena means that there is no such thing as "good" or "bad" action. Rather, good, and bad are descriptions of behaviors that the subject deems either good or bad. A conqueror or dictator doesn't care about moral judgements of others because he has a different moral system. The populace and the press might see this dictator as a ruthless and amoral monster, but the dictator sees them as weak and timid creatures. The dictator doesn't think he is bad because he defines what is good since he is powerful.

In many corrupt and impoverished countries around the world, there are people who wonder how their leaders could possibly be so inhumane and frivolous with the general well-being of the population. How it is that they are willing to gamble with their futures and their lives?

It is a deep puzzle that they simply cannot come to terms with. They cannot see the clear delineation that Nietzsche drew between two fundamentally different kinds of morality that operate on the world.

Nietzsche thought that master morality is essentially noble. And it is also open-minded, courageous, truthful, trustworthy, and honest about one's Self worth. Master morality originates in the "noble man" – with a natural conception of the good, and the idea of bad is then implied by what is not good. The noble man does not look for approval from others, he judges for himself. If something is harmful to him, then it is harmful, period.

Slave Morality

According to Nietzsche, masters create morality; slaves respond to master morality with their slave morality. Thus, slave morality is a reaction. It is based on a re-sentiment rather than on a sentiment – devaluing what the master values and the slave does not have. And just as master morality originates in the strong, slave morality finds its origins in the weak.

Since slave morality is a reaction to oppression, it frames its oppressors as villains. It is characterized by pessimism and cynicism. Slave morality does not aim at exerting one's will by strength, but by careful subversion. The goal of slave morality is not to become greater than the masters, but to make the masters slaves as well. The essence of slave morality is utility: the good is what benefits the entire community, not just the strong.

But Nietzsche saw this is a contradiction, since the powerful are outnumbered by the weak. The weak become powerful by corrupting the strong into believing that the causes of slavery (the will to power) are evil.

By saying that humility is voluntary, slave morality avoids admitting that they were forced to be humble. Biblical principles are then the codification of the plight of the slave to all of humankind, and thus enslaving the masters too. And democracy is the by-product of Christianity because of its obsession with freedom and equality.

Nietzsche hated democracy and notions of "equality of rights" and "sympathy with all sufferers," because he thought that this attempt to level the playing field stole from people the conditions that could make them great.

Oppression, poverty, violence, and severity of every kind were not evils to Nietzsche but the very foundations of transforming mediocrity to greatness, since the oppressed person is forced to fight, to be inventive, daring, and courageous.

To give them charity and equality would mean to quell their fires and to condemn them to a life of unfulfilled potential.

Christianity was a "slave morality" for Nietzsche because it called for the abandonment of pride, freedom, and Self-confidence.

Throughout history, there has always been a struggle between master and slave morality. The ancient Greek and Roman societies were based on master morality. But this master morality was defeated by Christianity, as slave morality spread to Europe.

Freud (1856-1939)

Dichotomy 6: Pleasure and Pain

Being rational, the individual will avoid buying anything that does not give them utils of pleasure and will buy items that bring the highest amount of pleasure. But this fundamental assumption, that humans are pleasure-seeking animals, contradicts the intellectual traditions that have survived. Man has found various ways to live, and not all of them give supremacy to the id. Some give more priority to the ego, while others are more subordinate to the superego.

The topic of pleasure was discussed extensively in ancient Greece, but it was not given the kind of reverence that you would expect, given the modern fascination with pleasure (even among academics). The Stoics, for example, did not think that pleasure was essential for life – they saw it as a hindrance to a virtuous existence.

Neither did the Cynics, nor the Platonists, who thought that life was worthless without contemplation. They believed that the human mind, rather than the body, was essential. Even the Epicureans, who are now synonymous with 'pleasure', and who we can identify as an early philosophical representation of the 'Pleasure Principle', were not hedonists in the modern colloquial sense. They were more interested in a sustainable pursuit of pleasure, which included contemplation, tranquility, and the freedom from fear.

Before the Epicureans, there were the Cyrenaics. They were an ultra-hedonistic school. They held that the only intrinsic good was pleasure. This was not the mere absence of pain, but the positively enjoyable momentary sensations. Among the Ancient Greeks, they are the closest instance of a philosophical school that can be thought of as hedonistic. But they understood the value of altruism and social obligations.

The school was founded by Aristippus of Cyrene. Aristippus, who was a student of

Socrates, was also the teacher of Theodorus the Atheist, who was an exponent of atheism and hedonism. The school died out less than a hundred years later, to be replaced by the Epicureans.

But the oldest tradition that promoted the pursuit of physical pleasure, were the ancient Babylonians. In the epic of Gilgamesh, soon after the invention of writing, Siduri gives us the following advice: "Fill your belly. Day and night make merry. Let days be full of joy. Dance and make music day and night.... These things alone are the concern of men."

The more modern philosophers have focused much less on the Greek mission of the "good life" and much more on existential, political, metaphysical, and ontological questions. So, one must assume, by default, that the hedonistic mission of the Cyreniacs have no place in their lives.

Recall that Adler took note of the inferiority complex in man, how man was motivated, not by what would maximize his success or pleasure, but what gave him the most anxiety or what made him feel weak and vulnerable. This is very different from the Darwinian idea of nature favoring the strong. The Adlerian insight is that, if anything, nature favors the weak, since they have much to prove – whereas the already powerful and "fit" may become complacent or reckless.

Like Freud, Jung carried on the spirit of Romanticism in his own works by emphasizing the importance of the shadow, man's darker impulses that are subconscious, and calling on those who are willing, not to disfigure and deform themselves in the pursuit of rational goals that are often socially conceived, but to look inwards, and to become more attuned to the "Self", and more comfortable with their own violent, irrational impulses, and to learn how to accept them as fundamental aspects of their identity. Contrary to the Enlightenment tradition, the Romantics have insisted that man should make peace with his Self-contradictions and dualities, and even to embrace them.

Jung emphasized the existence of the collective unconscious, which, in contrary to Freud's hypothesis that man is primarily driven by sexual instincts, recognizes in man the need to conform to ancient drives and impulses which have nothing to do with either pleasure or sexuality.

And it may be, that instead of pleasure, man is really motivated by the avoidance of pain. If we look at some religions and ancient philosophical ideologies, this seems to be a consistent idea.

In Ancient Greece, the Epicureans were much more concerned with the avoidance of pain (by emphasizing the need to eat small meals), than with the indulgence in pleasure.

A teaching in Christianity is to be wary of the pursuit of pleasure, and to accept that "life is suffering" and to see suffering as a virtue and as a pathway to salvation. Jesus was tortured and died on the cross – but his suffering was noble and heroic. If you are a Christian, your goal in life is to "imitate Christ", to suffer like he did, and to let go of your vain attempts at creating an earthly paradise.

In Buddhism, the goal is Nirvana, which is not an archipelago of pleasures, but is, in fact, a state of mind where suffering ceases to exist. Buddhism does not just tell you to avoid suffering, but it makes clear, that the biggest evil you can inflict on yourSelf is the constant pursuit of pleasure.

One way to explain these religions and philosophies that are against pleasure-seeking, psychologically, is by referring to the famous Aesop fable, where the fox solves the dilemma of being unable to reach for the grapes by finally proclaiming that they are too sour. Thus, the idea is not to stave off suffering through your actions, by trying to gain power, but to embrace suffering. And once you accept this idea psychologically, you are less prone to being consumed by your inevitable suffering in life.

All these systems of thought, by convincing people to let go of the pleasures of today, to accept suffering, and to learn how to become a friend to pain rather than a stranger to it, are aiming towards the same goal. They are priming the individual to adopt the notion of sacrifice. The individual either sacrifices present pleasure to avoid future pain or sacrifices an attachment to physical sensations for the well-being of their physical, psychological, and spiritual health.

Earlier, I discussed the Eastern ideas, which teach about the dissolution of the ego. If we think about the dichotomy between pleasure and pain, then we can see more clearly, what was being conveyed. The Eastern traditions gave priority to the elimination of pain, rather than the maximization of pleasure.

The modern world is the total opposite. The point of existence, if you are part of the modern economy, is to maximize the amount of pleasure you have, without any regard to pain. This dichotomy between pleasure and pain is important before I discuss the psychoanalytic ideas that emerged at the turn of the 19th century, because essentially, they were very much about pleasure and pain.

Freud's professional goal, as a therapist, was to relieve his patients of guilt and anxiety. At the time, society was far more conservative than it is now. People didn't act on their impulses, they repressed them. People had deeply held beliefs about what was considered appropriate and was not. His ideas, aimed at the upper-class who could afford his fees, were like a sedative against the patient's conscience, which prevented them from indulging in what they liked, and living a guilt-free existence. Unlike the Buddhists and the Eastern traditions, Freud saw inhibition rather than attachment as the main problem.

The Unmasking Trend

An importance source of Freudian thinking is the "unmasking trend" which took root in the 1880's. It is the systematic search for deception and

Self-deception and the uncovering of hidden truths. This trend started with the French moralists who thought of it as demystification. In his *Maxims*, La Rochefoucauld unmasked virtuous acts and attitudes as disguised manifestations of narcissism.

Schopenhauer described love as a mystification of the individual through the Genius of the Species, meaning that the qualities ascribed to the beloved are illusions, issuing from the unconscious will of the species.

Marx stated that the opinions of an individual, unknown to him, are determined by social class, which is determined by economic conditions. War and religion are "mystifications," in which the elite deceive the lower classes and themselves.

Nietzsche admired the French moralists and Schopenhauer and was a main proponent of "the unmasking trend." He investigated the many disguises of the will to power, and that of resentment which disguised itself as idealism and love of mankind. He emphasized that man had a need for fictions. In literature, unmasking was overdone, as can be seen in Ibsen's plays. Dostoevsky and Ibsen developed their "unmasking" psychology differently than the philosophers and psychologists.

Freud subscribed to Scientism, the idea that knowledge can only be acquired through science. But since science has limits, a large part of reality is unknowable, perhaps the greater part. Positivism should logically imply agnosticism, but Freud was a resolute atheist. His extreme positivist thinking led to a trend where its proponents expelled the "soul from psychology, vitalism from biology, and finality from evolution."

Klages, author of *The Biocentric Worldview*, noted that Nietzsche, a significant influence on Freud, belonged to the "unmasking trend."

Nietzsche's concern was to unveil how man is a Self-deceiving being, who constantly deceives his fellow men. And since man lies to himself more than to others, psychologists should base their conclusions on what people mean, and not from what they say or do.

For example, the Gospel's saying, "He that humbleth himself shall be exalted" should be "He that humbleth himself wishes to be exalted."

And what man thinks are his own convictions and feelings are often the remnants of assertions of his parents and ancestors.

In other words, we live from the folly and the wisdom of our ancestors. Nietzsche has relentlessly shown how every possible feeling, opinion, conduct, and virtue is rooted in Self-deception or an unconscious lie. The unconscious is the essential part of the individual, and consciousness is only an encoded expression of the unconscious, "a more or less fantastic commentary on an unconscious, perhaps unknowable, but felt text."

Dichotomy 7: Conscious vs Unconscious

Not only did Freud have a different take than the Eastern mystics with regards to pleasure, but since he heavily influenced by Romantic philosophers, he had an entirely different idea of the notion of Self. He thought there was no "individual" in the first place (that Is, an entity that cannot be divided). On the contrary, he thought that each person had multiple drives. And that these drives have their own goals, which the individual manifests.

One part of us desires pleasure, but another part of us wants to regulate it. To be more specific, Freud divided the psyche into three parts: the Id, Ego, and Superego. It was only the Id that had a relentless drive for pleasure.

Freud's the 'pleasure principle' describes man's desire to satisfy his primitive desires, including hunger and anger. If these needs are not met, a state of anxiety or tension follows. There are some needs that cannot be met because they are inappropriate in the moment, these needs don't disappear, but are repressed in the unconscious.

The Id is the most basic and animalistic part of the personality. And according to Freud, it is the only part of the personality that originated at birth. It is also the most repressed part of the psyche.

During childhood, the id is in full control. Children do not hesitate before satisfying their urges for food or pleasure. In fact, Freud realized that children seek the fastest way to satisfy their urges, they do not even think about the consequences of their behavior, or whether it is appropriate.

Freud previously thought that the mind had three layers: preconscious, unconscious, and conscious. Neuroses was a result of the conflict between the conscious and the unconscious. Language was an ego function; unconscious ideas were made preconscious through words.

The Id was not different from Freud's concept of the unconscious, but the word "unconscious" was now used to describe the id and parts of the ego and superego. The novel part of Freud's *The Ego and the Id* is the superego – the watchful, judging, and punishing agency in the individual. Freud concluded that the "Id is quite amoral, the ego strives to be moral, and the superego can be hyper-moral and cruel as only the Id can be."

Freud described the pitiful state of the ego, which was being bullied by other instincts. The main concern of psychotherapy would now be to help the ego by reducing these pressures and helping the ego gain strength.

Dichotomy 8: Individual vs Civilization

But when the child becomes an adult, and is a part of society, this kind of behavior is no longer tolerated. Here, the ego plays the vital role, because it keeps the demands of the Id in check. As a child grows up, the ego controls the urges of the Id. The ego wants to match behavior to the reality of the external world, it acts like a politician or schoolmaster, making exceptions in some cases, but is strict and authoritarian when the time calls for it. That is where a clash occurs between the ego and the Id.

Freud, in his later writings, came to acknowledge what Adler did before him – that children were more afraid of the outer world than of their inner world. This points to a fear of mortality and the unknown, and the same is found in the adult, who is fearful of falling to the clutches of machines, beasts, and men.

We think of love for mankind as the highest point we can achieve, but indiscriminate love is a problem since not everyone deserves love. Aim-inhibited love that exists between family members and friends solves the exclusiveness problem of instinctual love, while instinctual love leads to the creation of families.

Civilization aims to bring people together in large unities, but families will resist this – they will try to prevent man from integrating with the larger circle of life. Every young person's task is the leave the family, but this is difficult. Often cultures have employed rituals and rites of passage to accommodate this painful transition.

Why does the individual feel a sense of guilt? The Freudian answer may have something to do with the suppression of instincts by civilization. In the *Genealogy of Morals,* Nietzsche writes that our conscience is really nothing but the guilt we feel from not being able to act upon our instincts.

Speaking generally, there is no doubt but that even the justest individual only requires a little dose of hostility, malice, or innuendo to drive the blood into his brain and the fairness from it. The active man, the attacking, aggressive man is always a hundred degrees nearer to justice than the man who merely reacts; he certainly has no need to adopt the tactics, necessary in the case of the reacting man, of making false and biased valuations of his object. It is, in point of fact, for this reason that the aggressive man has at all times enjoyed the stronger, bolder, more aristocratic, and also freer outlook, the better conscience. On the other hand, we already surmise who it really is that has on his conscience the invention of the "bad conscience," — the resentful man!

*The Genealogy of Morals,
Friedrich Nietzsche*

The more we constrain ourselves, the more rules we follow, the more customs we adhere to, and the more we stifle Self-expression, the more we experience unpleasantness or guilt. It is a strange idea at first, but upon reflection, it fits in well with our intuitions about people.

You can imagine, for example, the Leonardo Di Caprio character in the *Wolf of Wallstreet*. He exhibits what Nietzsche called "the will to power"- he is interested in making money at all costs. He has made good friends with his aggressive nature, he allows it to prosper, and he uses it to fuel his ambition and his greed.

But then turn your imagination to a different image completely. Imagine an employee called Steve, working in a large bureaucratic corporation with a strict schedule. This man must dress up in a suit and tie every morning and must arrive perfectly on time. He must behave himself when he enters the office. No offensive jokes, no sexual innuendo, no expressions of aggression – merely compliance and politeness.

Who is more likely to harbor deep feelings of guilt, hatred, and resentment?

Freud gave Nietzsche a lot of credit for his apt observations on human nature. According to Ernest Jones, he often said of Nietzsche, "that he had a more penetrating knowledge of himself than any other man who ever lived or was likely to live."

What happens when someone tries to get rid of aggression? His aggression is internalized, and it never goes away. It is directed towards his own ego and is then taken over by the part of his ego that relates to his superego. And the tension between the harsh ego and the superego creates a sense of guilt – this is expressed as the need for punishment. This idea was expressed in a different way by Nietzsche in *The Genealogy of Morals*. Civilization achieves its goal by weakening the individual's ego – it makes people feel guilty when they do something they know is bad – even the intention alone can cause feelings of guilt.

Freud tells us that the extent of the power of the superego depends on fortune. When a man is fortunate, he is absent of the superego. But when man is misfortunate, his superego takes over, and he becomes extremely vigilant. In this condition, man interprets his fate as one where he is no longer loved by the highest power, and without this love, he looks for its representative in the superego – the same superego he neglected when things were going well.

At first, when man feared social authority, it was enough to renounce satisfaction to avoid punishment by an authority. But when there is fear of the superego, this renunciation is not enough since the wish itself to transgress cannot be concealed from the superego – this leads to guilt.

It is not that all men behave this way. The Israelites, despite god's continuous punishments only blamed themselves, whereas primitive man blames the object for not giving him what he wants. Primitive man does not blame himself.

In the civilized individual, the superego transfers anxiety to the ego – think of the aggressive instinct. Every instance of aggression given up is taken by superego and used against the ego – the child has internalized the father, the authority. A child's aggressiveness depends on the amount of punitive aggression he expects of his father, a leniently brought up child can acquire a strict conscience, but it is easy to see that the severity of parenting can influence the emergence of a powerful superego.

But the renunciation of instinct will relieve one from guilt from authority, but it will not relieve him of guilt altogether. In that sense, it no longer has a positive effect. The superego will cause man to be eternally unhappy and this problem can no longer be solved by an external authority. And there is a vicious cycle that man should contend with. The more you renounce, the more you will feel guilty, and this will lead to more renunciation. Conscience is the result of instinctual renunciation.

This presents us with the dilemma, that excessive Self-restraint which we exercise for the benefit of society, has a detrimental effect on our psychology. Civilized man exchanged part of his happiness for security. Neurosis is the result of the struggle between the libido and Self-preservation. Freud saw narcissism as a clue – it suggested that the ego too has a libido, and that the ego is the headquarters of instinct.

We cannot say that we naturally know what is bad. What is bad is sometimes desirable to the ego, and not injurious to it. Man's helplessness and dependence on others will make him succumb to what is good because he is afraid of punishment. What is bad is whatever threatens loss of love, and this also explains why there is no distinction in the amount of guilt one feels when he either manifests a bad action or merely thinks about doing so.

It is the fear of loss of love, and it is social anxiety that results from being caught in the act. In children, it is fear of losing parental love, and in adults, it is the loss of social love that is dreaded.

Sometimes, it is better to do what is bad for the benefit of the ego, for its own protection against the superego. The superego is the internal manifestation of the social authority. It creates anxiety within – the most virtuous people are the ones who have the most potent and violent superego.

According to Freud, man's sense of guilt stems from the Oedipus complex, the killing of the father by the brothers banded together in primitive times, a phenomenon Freud suspects did occur frequently. It was an act of aggression that wasn't suppressed but carried out.

The same act of aggression that was suppressed in the child is supposed to be the source of his guilt. It makes no difference whether when kills his father or not, one is guilty no matter what. Remorse after killing father came from feeling love and hate towards father – this was the origin of conscience, according to

Freud. Since this pattern repeated in the next generation, the sense of guilt was carried fort. Guilt results from the eternal struggle between Eros and Thanatos, and as mentioned before, between the ego and the superego.

Guilt isn't just in the subconscious; it appears in consciousness as a guilty conscience. As Nietzsche intuited, people have an unconscious need for punishment. Some people aren't aware of their sense of guilt, they only feel it as a sense of uneasiness or anxiety before doing certain things – the degree to which people are aware of their guilt is variable.

Sometimes, anxiety is so apparent that consciousness is consumed by it, other times, it is part of the subconscious and is not detectable by the consciousness. Religion has taken advantage of this sense of guilt, since they claim to redeem man from sin.

The superego is an agency that we have ascribed, it watches and judges the ego. It censors the ego. Guilt is the result of the ego fearing the superego's watchfulness. The need for punishment is an instinctual manifestation of the ego that is masochistic. It is the ego performing an erotic attachment to the superego. The sense of guilt predates the superego and conscience too. It is a recognition of the tension between the ego and the superego. One type of guilt comes from fear of external authority, the other from internal authority. Remorse contains the anxiety that operates behind the sense of guilt, it is a punishment, and can even include the need for punishment.

At one point, the sense of guilt was the aggression that was abstained from. But at another point (the killing of the primordial father), it came from carrying out the act. The superego altered the situation. Before that, guilt coincided with remorse. The omniscience of the superego eliminated the distinction between violence carried out and violence intended. Guilt from an evil deed is conscious, but guilt from an evil impulse is unconscious.

The energy of the superego carries the energy of the external authority, and/or it is using the aggression that was not used up. Closer reflection has reconciled this apparent contradiction. In each case we are dealing with an aggressiveness that was displaced inwards. Generally, they operate in unison. Any kind of frustration, or thwarted Self-satisfaction results in heightening the sense of guilt.

"Neurosis comes from unconscious sources of guilt. When an instinct is repressed, its libidinal elements turned into symptoms, its aggressive components into a sense of guilt."

Civilization and Discontents, Freud

Dichotomy 9: Eros vs Thanatos

While Eros versus Thanatos is an old idea, it is fundamental to understanding the development the civilization and the psyche. It is a general characteristic of life, but it fails to address the specifics.

Civilization serves Eros, which tries to create more people (more life) and man's natural aggression opposes this program. We don't know why Eros or Thanatos exist as primary drives; they simply do. The struggle between Eros and Thanatos characterizes the eternal battle in life. The inclination towards aggression is an instinct and is the greatest impediment to civilization.

Dichotomy 10: Happiness vs Unhappiness

In the first half of his career, Freud advanced the idea of the 'pleasure principle' which states that what people want is to become happy and remain so. They want to avoid pain and experience strong feelings of pleasure. And the pleasure principle dominates the mental apparatus from the start. But this intention is not included in the plans of creation or in nature. there is no possibility of it being carried through.

Happiness cannot exist independently. We can only be happy after the experience of unhappiness. Without a contrast, we cannot be happy. Here, we see the importance of polarity to our experience of a good life. We can never remain at a desirable end of any extreme (happiness, contentment, pleasure, satiation) without their contrasts (sadness, dissatisfaction, pain, hunger). This is a theme that will be important in understanding Jung, Freud's student.

We can never remain happy indefinitely, it is not part of our nature.

"What we call happiness can only result from the satisfaction of needs that have been damned up to such a degree, and it is by its nature an episodic phenomenon. When any situation that is derived by the pleasure principle is prolonged, it only produces a feeling of mild contentment. We are so made that we can derive intense enjoyment only from a contrast and very little from a state of things."

Civilization and Discontents, Sigmund Freud

Our biological makeup forces us to contend with this reality. However, unhappiness is easy to experience. There are three ways in which the individual perceives the world as an aggressive force. The first is the physical body that is prone to decay, the second is the external world which may destroy us at any moment, and the third is relations to other people which may deteriorate or end.

Egoism (happiness) and altruism (the need for social cohesion) are what underlies the development of the individual. The aim of happiness is pushed to the background by civilizational demands. In fact, the civilization does not care about individual happiness. The individual tries to satisfy both urges. But we can see that the urge to personal happiness and union with other human beings result in a constant struggle. The struggle between the individual and society is a dispute within the economics of the libido – how sexual energy is distributed.

The community also evolved a superego that oversees cultural development. The superego is the remnant of the personalities of great leaders with great minds, men who have found in themselves the most one-sided expression. These figures were often badly treated. The figure of Jesus Christ is an example.

The cultural superego and the personal superego set strict demands. The contents of the subconscious that arouses guilt in the individual, if risen to the surface, will be the same as that seen in society. Ethics should be thought as a therapeutic attempt, by means of the superego, something that has not been achieved by any other cultural activities, to limit aggression. But the question is how to get rid of man's predisposition towards aggression in the first place?

The criticisms of the superego according to Freud is that it takes no account of man's happiness, the ego's happiness. It is best to try to lower the demands of the superego, then. The cultural superego also doesn't care about the mental well-being of man. It merely commands without caring about whether it is possible for man to obey it, it assumes that man's ego can do anything, that his ego has unlimited control over the id. But this is a mistake, if more is demanded of man, a neurosis will develop, and he will become unhappy.

The assumption is that the civilizational path is a good one, but we don't know what consequences it will have on the individual, and whether he will be able to tolerate these consequences.

Freud's Transition

Dichotomy 6: Survival and Reproduction

Freud paid little attention to aggression in the first part of his work, when he thought that sexuality and Self-preservation were the two forces dominating man. After 1920, this changed. In *The Ego and the Id* (1923) and other writings, he introduced Eros and Thanatos.

He wrote…

> *"Starting from speculations on the beginning of life and from biological parallels I drew the conclusion that, besides the instinct to preserve living substance, there must exist another, contrary instinct seeking to dissolve those units and to bring them back to their primaeval, inorganic state. That is to say, as well as Eros there was an instinct of death."*
>
> *Sigmund Freud, 1930.*

Freud was the first modern psychologist who investigated the parts of the human experience that novelists and poets were interested in. He thought about the human passions (love, hate, ambition, greed, envy). And he tried to understand these passions through a scientific treatment of them. Freud stuck to the materialism of his teachers.

This was both respectable and limiting, because he was forced to explain all of human passions through the lens of the libido. As Fromm put it, aside from Self-preservation, all other human emotions were sublimations of or reaction formations against different manifestations of narcissistic, oral, anal, and genital libido.

Freud broke out of his initial scheme by presenting a new theory, which was key in the understanding of destructiveness. He concluded that life is not ruled by two egoistic drives (one for food, one for sex) but by two passions – love and destruction. These passions don't serve physiological survival in the same way that hunger and sexuality do. He called these passions Eros (life instinct) and Thanatos (death instinct). The names derive from gods in Greek mythology.

This classification breaks free numerous passions, such as the urge to love, be free, destroy, torture, and control, from their bondage to instincts.

Although Freud suggested that the power of the death instinct can be reduced, there was little that man could do to escape his tragic situation. He was destined for destruction because aggression was a deeply rooted impulse.

Instincts are a purely natural category (rooted in biology), while character-rooted passions contain sociobiology and history. While the latter do not directly serve physical survival, they are often more potent than instincts. And they form the basis for man's cultivation of meaning in life. They are behind dreams, art, religion, myth, and drama – everything that adds flavor to life.

Ellenberger, in *The Discovery of the Unconscious,* reminded us that before Freud, there was Schopenhauer who thought that the "goal of life is death." Another interesting feature of Freud's dichotomy is that the preservation instinct is itself an aspect of the death instinct, because it protects against accidental, externally caused death, so that the individual may die from internal causes. The individual would rather administer their own death blow, than allow himself to be swallowed up by the accidents of fate.

Recall that before coming up with the dichotomy (Eros versus Thanatos), Freud was a proponent of the primacy of the libido for many years. During that time, he rejected Adler's idea of an autonomous aggressive drive. Adler was another student of Freud who would go on to create his own school.

A part of the death instinct is diverted towards the external world and exists as destructiveness. There is internal destruction that occurs more slowly, but the aggression that is projected outwards comes at the expense of Self-destruction. Therefore, limiting external destruction will result in Self-destruction. Hence, why Fromm rightly points out that we would expect less outwardly aggressive humans and animals to die early or be more sick than outwardly aggressive members of their species, which we have no evidence for.

Think about how you sometimes sabotage your own plans. According to Freud, you only did so because there was energy left over from Thanatos that had not been directed at the world. Had you punched the person who served you coffee that morning, you would have stuck to your plans!

Freud suspected that people would doubt the existence of the death instinct, and this is not surprising to him. But he found it to be a great compliment to his previous theories about the ego.

For instance, sadism can fulfill the death instinct without Eros and be accompanied with narcissistic enjoyment, fulfilling the ego's wish for omnipotence. When the instinct of destruction is directed towards objects, it satisfies the ego, and gives it a feeling of control over nature.

The idea of the death instinct had precursors (other than Schopenhauer), Von Schubert was among the Romantics who expressed it clearly – mainly as a wish in the latter part of life, to die. Novalis said that "life is for the sake of death." Novalis thought that the antithesis to death was the instinct of organization (culture, language, philosophy).

How were Freud's ideas received by his audience?

The ideas in *Beyond the Pleasure Principle* had mixed reviews among psychoanalysts, but those presented three years later in *The Ego and the Id* was much more successful. Freud defined the ego as "the coordinated organization of mental processes in a person." In the latter book, he defined the mind as consisting of id, ego, and superego. He wrote that the ego had a conscious and unconscious element. Perception and motor control constituted the conscious ego, while dreams and repression constituted the unconscious ego.

But Freud's great discovery was that the cause of so many mental illnesses was man's inability to accept his own memories, emotions, and impulses. Repression is a defensive tactic that we automatically use to protect ourselves and our Self-image.

Each animal is given a sense of value by its genetic programming, but humans are different, we need to cultivate our own sense of Self-worth. Man should learn to repress his smallness in the world, and failure to live up to its rules and its codes. He must repress the insecurities and anxieties of his parents to protect his assuredness in himself. And yet, this repression is the cause of many ailments. In other words, man is forced to repress so much to function, but in doing so, he causes himself much harm.

As mentioned before, in the latter half of his career, Freud concluded that that Eros is more than sexual instinct, that it exists in every living cell and drives the living substance to constitute larger beings, it postpones death in this way. The death instinct is the tendency for the living substance to return to a state of inanimate matter. But the two drives are primordial, they are inseparable, and life is a compromise between Eros and Thanatos until the latter prevails. Freud hoped the biology would confirm these speculations in scientific terms.

According to Fromm, Freud made an important step forward here, he transcended the purely physiological-mechanistic theory he had first drawn up and had created an innovative biological theory that considered the organism as a whole and analyzed the biological triggers of love and hate.

But his theory had problems since it is largely unsubstantiated. In addition, his hypothesis contradicts what we know about animal behavior. Freud didn't just think Thanatos existed in humans, but that it was a force that existed in all animals. This implies that animals should express this instinct against themselves or others. So, we should expect to find more illness or early death in less outwardly aggressive animals, and vice versa, but there is no data to support this claim.

Freud, in opting to maintain dualistic elegance (survival and reproduction, Eros and Thanatos), sacrificed the explanatory power of his theories

---

Man cannot live as nothing but an object, as dice thrown out of a cup; he suffers severely when he is reduced to the level of a feeding or propagating machine, even if he has all the security he wants. Man seeks for drama and excitement; when he cannot get satisfaction on a higher level, he creates for himself the drama of destruction.

The Anatomy of Human Destructiveness, Erich Fromm

Fromm, for his part, did not think that destruction preceded man or was a force that existed in all animals. Clearly, human cruelty was unique to humans. Animals were not cruel or evil in the way humans are. So, Freud's theory in the end makes an unsubstantiated claim and does not explain the problem of malicious aggression. Fromm thought that malicious aggression was uniquely human, not for biological reasons, but because man has a need for drama and excitement.

These destructive passions, according to Fromm, do not become powerful only when the more essential needs are satisfied. They are at the root of human existence. People have committed suicide because they have failed to realize their passions for love, power, fame, or revenge. No one commits suicide because of a lack of sexual satisfaction or lack of food.

In other words, these non-instinctual passions make life worth living. They transform man from a mere animal into a hero. This is a different interpretation from Ernest Becker, who thought that these human strivings were man's unconscious and conscious attempts at masking their own mortality. To Fromm, these passions are not the result of a delusion, but an essential part of a meaningful existence as a human being.

To Fromm, malicious aggression is a mistake or a perversion, but nonetheless, it belongs to humans, and only humans. It is man's mistaken attempt to make sense of life.

These considerations by no means imply, however, that destructiveness and cruelty are not vicious; they only imply that vice is human. They are indeed destructive of life, of body and spirit, destructive not only of the victim but of the destroyer himself. They constitute a paradox: they express life turning against itself in the striving to make sense of it.

The Anatomy of Human Destructiveness, Erich Fromm

Jung (1875-1961)

Dichotomy 11: Ease vs Difficulty

Freud had a star pupil, Carl Jung. There are many ideas of Jung that I will discuss in this book, but first, I will mention Jung's explanation for why the repression that Freud spoke about exists.

According to Jung. when man became aware of sin, he became capable of repression. Secrets are created – since anything that is concealed is a secret. But secrets are difficult to deal with. If you hold too many, they will destroy you, but to maintain sanity and differentiate yourSelf as an individual, you need to hold on to some. Jung stipulated that some kinds of neurosis arose from too many secrets, while others from too little.

Repenting is a rite of passage. Men who refuse to do so, and instead defend their pride, will face an impenetrable wall that will shut them out from living properly among other men. As was foretold by the Greeks, "Give up what thou hast, and then thou wilt receive."

Jung then takes us through some of the fundamental problems of psychotherapy.

It is necessary but difficult to acknowledge that radiant works of beauty do not have pure origins. He explains, "No thoughtful person will deny that Salomon Reinach's explanation of the Last Supper in terms of primitive totemism is fraught with meaning; nor will he object to the incest-theme being pointed out in the myths of the Greek divinities.

> *"It is painful there is no denying it - to interpret radiant things from the shadow-side, and thus in a measure reduce them to their origins in dreary filth. But it seems to me to be an imperfection in things of beauty, and a weakness in man, if an explanation from the shadow-side has a destructive effect."*

Jung wrote that some choose to rebel against Freud's ideas about repression, because we naively and childishly believe that "there can be heights without corresponding depths, and which blinds us to the really" final" truth that, when carried to extremes, opposites meet." The other mistake, that even Freud himself has made, was to think that because works of beauty had shadow origins – that they were any less radiant. "Yet the shadow belongs to the light as the evil belongs to the good, and vice versa."

Jung thinks that most people who find it easy to integrate socially are tortured by their desires (the pleasure principle).

People who are unsuccessful – those who have failed socially, long to be "normal." But for people who have above average ability who have never found it challenging to fit in, "normal" for them "signifies the bed of Procrustes, unbearable boredom, infernal sterility and hopelessness." You can only become satisfied and fulfilled by what you do not yet have. And you cannot be satisfied by what you have in abundance.

"To be a socially adapted being has no charms for one to whom to be so is mere child's play. Always to do what is right becomes a bore for the man who knows how, whereas the eternal bungler cherishes the secret longing to be right for once in some distant future."

Jung believed that – in addition to a present day, personal consciousness, we need a supra-personal consciousness, in other words – a collective consciousness that predates the individual human being and is "open to a sense of historical continuity." Many neuroses are caused by people's childish pursuit of rational enlightenment and ignore their "own religious promptings." The issue goes beyond dogma and creed. "A religious attitude is an element in psychic life whose importance can hardly be overrated."

Jung emphasizes the importance of thinking about life in stages. When you are young, it is important to learn the necessary skills that will allow you to become socially useful. Since you haven't achieved anything yet, it is important for you to shape your conscious ego as well as you can. It is unlikely to feel anything that is active within yourSelf that is different from your will. You must feel that you are a man of will, and get rid of everything else within yourSelf, or think of it as succumbing to your will. You will not be able to socially integrate properly without convincing yourSelf of this illusion.

According to Jung, achievement is a good surrogate goal, but is limited. When you are young it is useful to focus on achievement than to wander around contemplating complex metaphysical ideas, but ultimately, achievement will be unable to provide you with something you crave more deeply.

Achievements "may be our lode-stars in the adventure of extending and solidifying our psychic existences - they may help us in striking our roots in the world; but they cannot guide us in the development of that wider consciousness to which we give the name of culture."

As you get older, a deeper spiritual understanding becomes necessary. You don't need to educate your conscious will. You don't care about being socially useful anymore. You are now more interested in investigating the meaning of your life, and it would be possible to do so by learning to experience your "own inner being."

"To the psychotherapist an old man who cannot bid farewell to life appears as feeble and sickly

116

*as a young man who is unable
to embrace it."*

Jung relates "passing through stages" to the story of Adam and Eve – the symbolic fall of man in the Bible. The birthplace of tragedy for man is marked by his escape from his primitive unconscious state to a conscious one. And similarly, human beings, when going through different stages of life will have made the transition from unconscious, joyful youth to conscious, guilt-ridden adults.

"Every one of us gladly turns away from his problems; if possible, they must not be mentioned, or, better still, their existence denied. We wish to make our lives simple, certain and smooth-and for that reason problems are tabu. We choose to have certainties and no doubts-results and no experiments-without even seeing that certainties can arise only through doubt, and results through experiment."

Modern Man's Search for a Soul, Carl Jung

Jung emphasizes the importance of challenging ourselves and encountering the unknown. One of his observations is that people who have had to struggle for their existence do not seem to have psychological problems, which are much more common in those who have had a comfortable upbringing. And such problems do not seem to be detectable externally, as it is possible to excel in the external world and yet experience a strained inner life. These problems may relate to inferiority complexes.

However, Jung emphasizes that these complexes need not be so destructive. While they do represent inferiority, they do not necessarily indicate inferiority. They only point to an unresolved conflict but can be the stimulus you need to exert greater effort, and potentially achieve more than you would have otherwise. In that sense, you wouldn't want to do away with complexes.

If people didn't have them, psychic life would come to a "fatal standstill." Complexes indicate "the unresolved problems of the individual, the points at which he has suffered a defeat, at least for the time being, and where there is something, he cannot evade or overcome - his weak spots in every sense of the word."

Indeed, Jung thinks that the point of life isn't to resolve every problem, but to embark on an uphill battle. "If it should for once appear that they (problems) are, this is the sign that something has been lost. The meaning and design of a problem seem not to lie in its solution, but in our working at it incessantly."

Recall Freud's assertion that the individual who experiences a strict and difficult upbringing is more likely to have a punitive and powerful superego.

Jung and Freud were essentially saying that difficulties impose upon the young person an internal voice that demand from them to get their act together, and to become competent. For these individuals, it will be easier to fit into socially useful roles, and less likely to experience psychic disturbances.

As the individual transitions from youth to adulthood, he is given a reality check. His presuppositions about the world are challenged.

Jung wrote that if "the individual is sufficiently well prepared, the transition to a professional career may take place smoothly. But if he clings to illusions that contradict reality, then problems will surely arise." The individual may have unrealistic expectations of the future, and a radical underestimation of the difficulties he will face. It may be the case that people who have been given this reality check earlier in life – by being raised in harsh circumstances – are more likely to circumvent delayed disillusionment.

A part of us wants to stay young and remain in our monistic phase – where we can only identify with our ego. This is a narrower level of consciousness than the dualistic stage, where the individual can come to terms with what is alien and strange. He can accept that he has a contradictory nature – his "also I."

"Whoever protects himself against what is new and strange and thereby regresses to the past, falls into the same neurotic condition as the man who identifies himself with the new and runs away from the past. The only difference is that the one has estranged himself from the past, and the other from the future."

Modern Man's Search for a Soul, Carl Jung

But the reality of the inner man is undeniable, and we will need to eventually discover him. We will need to descend into the depths of our psyche and discover that part of us that has contradictory goals to our conscious Self and is strange and hostile to us. But do not expect to get rewarded for these efforts by society. Achievement and not personality is rewarded. However, a stronger inner life is the most important precursor to success in the external world.

> *"Ideas spring from a source that is not contained within one man's personal life. We do not create them; they create us. Knowledge rests not upon truth alone, but upon error also."*
>
> *Modern Man's Search for a Soul, Carl Jung*

Jung criticizes Freud and the modern, rational man for treating the issue of God too frivolously. Jung maintains that even the idea of faith to the modern man is a misconception.

> *"The strange thing is that man will not learn that God is his father." That is what Freud would never learn, and what all those who share his outlook forbid themselves to learn. At least, they never find the key to this knowledge. Theology does not help those who are looking for the key, because theology demands faith, and faith cannot be made: it is in the truest sense a gift of grace.*

> *"We have now discovered that it was intellectually unjustified presumption on our forefathers' part to assume that man has a soul; that that soul has substance, is of divine nature and therefore immortal; that there is a power inherent in it which builds up the body, supports its life, heals its ills and enables the soul to live independently of the body; that there are incorporeal spirits with which the soul associates; and that beyond our empirical present there is a spiritual world from which the soul receives knowledge of spiritual things whose origins cannot be discovered in this visible world."*
>
> *Modern Man's Search for a Soul, Carl Jung*

Jung shows that while it may have been presumptuous for our ancestors to posit the existence of immaterial souls, our modern interpretation of reality is no less presumptuous. And in fact, the concepts that scientists have created – and all men assume they understand are no less strange or bewildering than ancient ideas about spirituality. For example, many people take for granted that matter can produce spirit, that apes can give rise to human beings, that from some kind of harmonious interplay of hunger, love, and power, Kant's *Critique of Pure Reason* was written; that brain cells create thoughts, and that all of this could not possibly have been any other way.

What or who, indeed, is this all-powerful matter? It is once more man's picture of a creative god, stripped this time of his anthropomorphic traits and taking the form of a universal concept whose meaning everyone presumes to understand."

Modern Man's Search for a Soul, Carl Jung

Sometimes, we don't know why we behave the way we do. Many people don't know why the body needs salt, but they demand it, nevertheless. It's an instinctive need. And the same can be said about belief in the continuance of life. People have held these ideas from time immemorial.

The thyroid was once considered a useless organ because no one understood its function. So is the case with the appendix more recently. It would be just as short-sighted of us to presume that primordial images or ideas are senseless.

"Do we ever understand what we think? We only understand that thinking which is a mere equation, and from which nothing comes out but what we have put in. That is the working of the intellect. But beyond that there is a thinking in primordial images-in symbols which are older than historical man; which have been ingrained in him from earliest times, and, eternally living, outlasting all generations, still make up the groundwork of the human psyche."

Modern Man's Search for a Soul, Carl Jung

The scientific answer to what happens after a person dies, for example, does not exist. We do not know one way or another. We don't even know where our own ideas come from.

Useful Fictions

There is the idea of "useful fictions" which are stories that benefit you regardless of whether they are factually true. These may come in the form of inter-subjective truths, such as money, which drives the capitalist system. There is nothing "real" about money other than the fact that everybody believes in its value. And there are other useful fictions that do not need to be shared with the collective but can be useful to the individual himself.

In *Man's Search for Meaning*, Frankl emphasized the point that even in the worst conditions, men who had something meaningful to work for, whether it be the publishing of a book, or the reunion with a loved one, were able to put up with the worst conditions of imprisonment during war. Even though these events may never happen, the belief in them happening, can imbue a sense of optimism and resilience in the individual in the face of adversity.

The sovereignty of the individual is an idea, which, if discarded, would lead to social chaos.

We have these beliefs, implicitly or explicitly, and they drive our behavior. They give us stories that we can tell ourselves and others, and it is these stories – that are underlined with a religious substructure or system of axiomatic presuppositions – that we inherit from ancestors and pass down to future generations.

What Jung discovered was that one category of stories that are biologically inherited are ancient myths – and these myths inform our modern stories such as "the sovereignty of the individual." The Christian myths are an articulation of ancient patterns of behavior that have led to the flourishing of society. The idea that all men are equal before God, regardless of their position in society or their race, is a non-rational archetypal idea that informs our legal and political systems.

It as if the human organism has slowly been gaining Self-knowledge, but in a process that has been loosely structured and difficult to fully understand, religions have been able to communicate these implicit presuppositions through stories.

Dichotomy 12: Good vs Evil

The controversial aspect of Jung's thought is not merely his dabbling in alchemy and mysticism, which he explains as an attempt to find a connection with Gnostic ideas. While he denied it himself, there is no doubt that Jung was greatly influenced by Gnostic teachings. There are some authors, such as Hoeller, who suggest that Jung's depth psychology was derived from a Gnostic experience he experienced over three nights, when he wrote *The Seven Sermons to the Dead.*

The Gnostics were a heretical sect of Christianity who were persecuted by all the major religions. The Gnostics thought that this world was created, not by an all-loving God, but by a demiurge, or evil spirit, that humans existed for no other reason than to provide these demiurges spiritual insight and but that there was an essential holiness at the center of each human soul. The Gnostics also believed that each good quality has its bad side, and nothing that is good can come into the world without directly producing a corresponding evil. This teaching is in great conflict with conventional Christian teachings, which state that good and evil are clearly distinct, and that the human being should cleanse himself of any association with evil.

There is difficulty in admitting that we have good or bad natures – especially in a secular age. It is easier to deny the existence of evil, to rationalize it out of existence. Then, you can never be found guilty of either good or evil but are merely a product a biologically determined inclinations. In other words, you evolved that way, it's not your fault. But equally, the same logic can be applied to social influences. A serial killer can be accused of being guilty because he was brainwashed by others, or that harsh childhood circumstances led him to develop an apathy and indifference to human life.

Whether the cause is biological or environmental, the secular mind tends to (but not always) avoid thinking in good vs evil terms.

The repercussions of this way of thinking are numerous and problematic. When you see things as opposites, then you are also very much concerned with stark divisions. You are more likely to judge some people as totally good and others as totally evil. You will miss the subtle truths of reality, as is symptomatic of the left-brain dominated vision.

This simplistic vision of reality will spur you on towards constantly seeking pleasure to avoid pain, while not realizing that the persistent chase of pleasure is itself the cause of pain. Since the left-brained person, who is identified with their will, or their ego, sees things as good or bad, they cannot accept a holistic vision of reality whereby there is deep interplay between opposites. Jung and the Gnostics believed that the unbridled motivation for good conceals a deep evil, while a relentless pursuit of evil contains something essentially good. For example, the excessive emphasis on good manners, politeness, and the concealment of one's real opinion, is on the surface, the mark of a good character. But underneath, there is brewing resentment, hatred, and frustration, which will inevitably find its outlet.

The incessant need for order, so that moral conflict can be avoided, is the breeding ground for moral chaos. We can see why without much thinking: too much order will lead to excessive oppression from bureaucracies, and law enforcement, and so on. It is often the most virtuous societies that are also the most repressive and violent.

The controversies that have surrounded the world's religious institutions, for example, may not be a coincidence after-all. It is here, that we can learn something from psychoanalysis, and from the study of human nature as it is, rather than how it is ordered to be by political authorities disguised as mediators of God. That is not to say that religious people are evil. I am making precisely the opposite point. Because so many religious people are close to saintliness in their orientation and behavior, as far as it can be attained by human beings, there is the inevitable fall into evil for some, in the same way that the relentless pursuit of pleasure often ends in pain. The best advice would be, "be good, but not too good."

In *Modern Man's Search for a Soul*, Jung makes a powerful case against the scientific rationalist. He attempts to dismantle the false certitude behind our modern scientific presuppositions, and asks us to approach deep, difficult problems with an open mind. And most importantly, he asks us to not dismiss ancient or primordial people, for they are not less rational than we are, but only start from different presuppositions.

Given that civilization causes the repression of primal impulses, man must find a solution – sublimation.

In *Civilization and its Discontents*, notice how Freud's thesis focused on the essential dilemma of being connected and separated at the same time. We are connected because we exist in mutually beneficial relationships with others in society. At the same time, the "others" seek to restrict our freedom, and sometimes, actively seek to cause us harm. In the same way, the person who is too identified with good, is also disconnected from others in society who are not good. And it is this disconnection which is the cause of a repressed capacity for evil.

In modern capitalistic society, the individual feels especially disconnected, isolated, and disenfranchised when they have failed to achieve financial success or fame. *In Man's Search for Himself*, Rollo May alludes to the movie *Death of a Salesman*, starring Dustin Hoffman. Hoffman is a traveling salesman for a large corporation and lives his entire life in the pursuit of one goal: to be liked by everyone. It is a motto he prides himself in and teaches his two sons to internalize. The tragedy is that in the end, he fails to do even that. After reaching a retirement age, he is let go by his employer. Overnight, he loses his livelihood and sense of meaning. Not only was he dispensable, but clearly, he was not *really* liked.

Hoffman's character desperately wanted to feel connected, and for a while, he did. But ultimately, the ruthless demands of the "system" disconnected him from that which he felt connected to. Civilization imbues the individual with purpose before revoking it.

But even the individual who is not eventually estranged, experienced a sense of alienation from their own instincts. For the flourishing of civilization to be possible, the individual must reign in their natural instincts, but this is never without a price.

Propaganda

If man meditates on the premises underlying Christianity, he will either choose to implicitly believe or accept that he does not understand. While state truths and scientific truths are easy to understand – religious truths are not. But even if he rejects religious truths, he will still have a religious instinct, and it will be filled by other kinds of gods, according to Jung.

It is misleading to dismiss instincts as blind and irrational – they are the most fundamental parts of who we are. Because of their ancient roots, they are a more real part of us, in a sense, than our organs. Jung theorized that the instinct is original and hereditary, and much older and conservative that the body's form.

We need to create a better context within which our instincts can better operate – through the formulation of more suitable ideas for our new environment. But for our instincts to be able to operate in our modern environment, we need to reshape them. The original purpose of philosophy was to provide a framework for us to live our lives – not to exist as a detached, dry, dead, academic discipline.

Our reverence for the "word" or Logos has its origins in Christianity. It was a tool for the transmission of a divine message, but after centuries of education – the "word" has attained universal validity. The "state" and "society" are substitutes for our conceptions of the divine.

"No one seems to notice that the veneration of the word, which was necessary for a certain phase of historical development, has a perilous shadow side. The moment the word, as a result of centuries of education, attains universal validity, it severs its original link with the divine person. There is then a personified Church, a personified State; belief in the word becomes credulity, and the word itself an infernal slogan capable of any deception. With credulity come propaganda and advertising to dupe the citizen with political jobbery and compromises, and the lie reaches proportions never known before in the history of the world."

The Undiscovered Self, Carl Jung

Man has identified with his conscious knowledge of himself – at the expense of the unconscious. He has estranged himself from his instincts through his capacity to learn. Learning – while responsible for the "transformation of human modes of behavior and the altered conditions of our existence" is also responsible for the "numerous psychic disturbances and difficulties occasioned by man's progressive alienation from his instinctual foundation."

In an interesting section about Ellul's work on propaganda, Lasch notes that propaganda does not use facts to support an argument, but to exert emotional pressure. Advertising does the same. But in both cases, the point is not to make the emotional appeal obvious or direct – the emotional appeal is made through the facts themselves which give the person the illusion that they are being "informed."

Since the propagandist knows that educated people relish facts and the illusion of being informed, they do not use high-sounding slogans, or appeal to fantastic ideas. They do not call for heroism or sacrifice or reminds his audience of the glorious past. They merely stick to the "facts." This marks the union of propaganda and "information."

Dichotomy 13: Sublimation vs Repression

What is the Self-knowledge that Jung alludes to?

Sublimation is a way for the individual to overcome the sense of alienation from his instincts that society imposes on him. And perhaps, this takes care of aggressive and sexual instincts in a productive way. But what about man's other instincts?

If we take Jung's argument seriously, and we accept that man has a religious instinct that is no less real than his other instincts, or his physical constitution, and no less ancient or primal, then what should he do? And if he chooses to ignore such an instinct, what are the consequences?

In the next section of this book, we will explore man's narcissism, and the different arguments for why the turning away from the religious instinct may lead us straight towards narcissism. As Nietzsche succinctly put it long ago, after declaring the death of God, "must we not become Gods ourselves?"

God is dead. God remains dead. And we have killed him. How shall we comfort ourselves, the murderers of all murderers? What was holiest and mightiest of all that the world has yet owned has bled to death under our knives: who will wipe this blood off us? What water is there for us to clean ourselves? What festivals of atonement, what sacred games shall we have to invent? Is not the greatness of this deed too great

*for us? Must we ourselves not
become gods simply to appear
worthy of it?*

The Joyful Science, Nietzsche

What is the difference between sublimation and repression? Sublimation occurs when a drive's primary aim is substituted for a secondary aim that allows the expression of the drive in a way that is congruent with the master drive. Repression is what happens when a drive is denied its aim and is split off from other drives in that its aims are not integrated with the aim of other drives.

How should we deal with our innate instincts as they arise? Freud proposed that libidinal energy cannot be cut off (as the Buddha thought) but can be replaced by energy for a higher aim, and one that is not rooted in instinctual desires: sublimation.

No individual is ultimately well-adjusted, as Freud observed, because there is an essential conflict that takes place between the individual and society, between unbridled instinct and social norms. The answer to this conflict, according to Freud was sublimation – the redirection of libidinal energy towards socially beneficial pursuits. It was society's ingenious creation, an outlet that allowed the individual to express their primal drives, peacefully and productively.

Imagine a sadist who would have been destined to end up in prison because of his insatiable desire to inflict pain on his fellow human beings, instead becomes a surgeon or a dentist – that is, gets paid for being inhumane. Or think of the case of the professional NFL athlete who knocks people unconscious for a living.

These individuals, according to the theory of sublimation, are granted a socially permissible expression of their instincts. Similarly, the misfit standup comedian filled with hatred, or the angry novelist, or the rage-filled musician, or Jordan Belfort from *The Wolf of Wallstreet* is permitted to express themselves in a productive way.

A study in 2013[i] showed that Protestants were more likely to sublimate their taboo feelings into creative activities, and that people who had sexual problems related to anxieties over taboo desires were more likely to have creative accomplishments than those who did not. These studies may be the first experimental evidence for sublimation.

The theory of sublimation is informed by Freud's conception of id, ego, and superego. The id is the primitive part of our personality, and the ego emerges later during childhood – the ego reigns in the id and makes it conform to the demands of the real world. The superego, or the moral arbitrator, constantly strives to make us behave according to higher ethical standards. The ego's job is to mediate between the id and the superego.

One way the ego can reduce the anxiety created by our primitive feelings is through sublimation – a mature and constructive way for people to manifest these feelings.

Freud stumbled upon the idea of sublimation by accident. He got it when reading a well-known travel book, *The Harz Journey*, by the poet Heinrich Heine. The poet recalls meeting a great German surgeon called Johann Friedrich Dieffenbach, who used to be a sadistic little boy – he loved to cut off the tails off stray dogs for pleasure, but as an adult, he transformed into a brilliant surgeon who made pioneering discoveries in his field.

Freud believed that many great achievements in politics, the arts, and the sciences stemmed from a desire for compensation – for example, a politician who campaigns for the poor may be sublimating the greed he felt when he was younger.

He notes that far from becoming nihilistic because of our unmet needs, we manage to transform into functional adults – most of the time. He reminds us that we started out as babies – a time when we believed that not getting exactly what we wanted whenever we pleased would bring about the end of the world. We were Self-centered and found it difficult to be generous to others, but we managed to substitute our narcissistic aims for more ethical ones.

Freud has noted the difficulty of separating symptoms from sublimations and similarly, sickness from health – there isn't a sharp distinction between normal and neurotic people. Neuroticism substitutes for repression and is necessary for the normal transition from childhood to adulthood. In other words, everyone is somewhat neurotic, but what makes someone pathologically so, is having a high number of neurotic symptoms – and only that would justify labeling this person as "ill" or having a "constitutional inferiority."

There are destructive ways of manifesting libidinal energy according to Freud, these include repression, displacement, denial, reaction formation, intellectualization, and projection.

The Buddha would have agreed with Freud, that the total repression of instinct was not a tenable strategy. The Buddha's perspective would have condemned a life devoted to satisfying the cravings of the id, since he believed that sense pleasures are low, common, and unprofitable. On the other hand, to search for happiness through denial or asceticism or denial is painful, unworthy, and unprofitable.

To dissolve the sense of Self in pleasurable experiences is only a temporary refuge from suffering and giving free reign to the emotions is not effective. Attacking the body and subjecting the Self to strict rules did not relieve suffering, nor did the denial of emotions.

The correct approach, according to the Buddha, is to find a balance between these two approaches.

It required the alignment of eight specific factors of mind and behavior: understanding, thought, speech, action, livelihood, effort, mindfulness, and concentration. When these factors were established, they led to the Path to Cessation.

Unlike Freud, who thought everything was about the libido, Jung didn't agree that sublimation was the redirection of sexual energy, he thought that it was more mystical. Jung thought that there was much more to the unconscious than mere aggressive and sexual impulses – this is more in line with the Buddhistic perspective on the unconscious.

Jung thought that Freud was trying to make sublimation fit a rationalistic, scientific worldview when it didn't, and that Freud invented the idea to save us from our terrifying unconscious. For Jung, transformation is a social duty. While Freud's idea of sublimation was purely materialistic, Jung recognized the transcendental potential of the psyche, he saw it as something to be respected – as something mysterious.

The French psychoanalyst Jacques Lacan thought that as human beings, we all experience a vacuum, and we try to fill it with relationships with other people, objects, or experiences – but never quite getting there. Das Ding ("The Thing" in German) was a lost object that man was forever chasing after. Sometimes, the individual might be tricked by his psyche into believing that his needs could be satisfied in an enduring way by a person, thing, or experience. But one never finds Das Ding, only its pleasurable associations.

Lacan has noted the difficulty in properly defining sublimation, but Lacanian sublimation is built on the idea of Das Ding. Lacan thinks that these objects, which are philosophical, aesthetic, or credal are representative of Das Ding, and that the pleasure principle leads the subject from one signifier to another, thus relieving psychic tension.

Think of an intellectual moving from one idea to the next, or an artist who paints one canvas after another, or a person who moves from relationship to relationship, constantly trying to satisfy this urge that will never go away. Man creates his own support system; he finds the signifiers that delude him into believing that he has overcome the emptiness of Das Ding.

Nietzsche also had views on sublimation. Nietzsche thought of individuals as being collections of drives. But most modern humans – members of the denigrated herd, are simply disorganized collections of competing drives, with these drives exchanging superiority at different times.

But Nietzsche's ideal weaker drives are not suppressed or shackled. Nietzsche thought that sublimation applied to both sexual and aggressive instincts – that sublimation came from inhibition or an intellectual process. "Good actions are sublimated evil ones."

Both Nietzsche and Freud saw sublimation as a mark of health. Nietzsche saw it as a pathway towards a unified Self, and while Freud defined health in utilitarian terms or relative happiness, Nietzsche measured it in terms of freedom from bitterness and the conflicting urges between drives, he measured it in terms of abundant expressive energy and Self-overcoming.

And Nietzsche, unlike Freud, did not see the need for an ego. He thought we have conflicting drives, but none were regulated by an ego. Freud said that falling in love is a humble act since the person falling in love must forfeit a part of his narcissism.

Jung conceived of the libido as a non-specific psychic energy that adjusts itself to the situation whether it requires sex, love, or the intellect. Freud disliked how Jung weakened the link between the idea of libido and sexuality – particularly the 'infantilism of sexuality.' Freud could not accept that the Oedipal Complex was merely symbolic.

Introversion was not a sign of neurosis for him, but it did promote it. Introversion marks the turning away from possibilities of real satisfaction, and towards an obsession of object or idea that is seen as innocent. The introvert is not yet neurotic, but is in an unstable situation, where his neglect of the difference between reality and fantasy, may lead to neurosis – especially if he does not find an outlet for his stored-up libido.

Dichotomy 14: Persona vs Self

Individuation

In *Individuation and Narcissism*, Mario Jacoby explains the differences between the great psychoanalytic thinkers of our time, including Freud, Jung, Neumann, Kohut – particularly their thoughts on narcissism, why it develops, and the signs that it manifests. In addition, there is a thorough discussion of the process of individuation, how it was arrived at through multiple, independent paths as a solution to many modern psychological problems, and which problems occur because of the failure to individuate.

Jung strove towards individuation personally. Earlier in life, he nearly became an artist, but he identified the anima in this case as the cause of this motivation. He was able to restrain himself and pursue a more critically minded path. His special talent for grasping symbolic material allowed him to simultaneously maintain critical ego functions and to put these in the service of a relatively objectified scientific research.

Were his ideas on individuation too subjective? It depends on who you ask. While his theories were grounded in plenty of research, they were derived from mythology, popular belief, mysterious personal experiences, and alchemy. Many thinkers have accused Jung of pushing a quasi-religious brand of mysticism, wrapping his messages in pseudo-insightful ambiguous jargon. But we should be fair to Jung. The previous section, which covered *The Undiscovered Self*, demonstrates a more pragmatic minded Jung, who clearly saw the problems of his age. In this section of the book, I will give the reader a brief overview of Jung's other contributions.

Individuation is the big idea laid forth by Jung, which ultimately underpins all his other concepts. Jung defined individuation as the process by which individuals became differentiated from the group – from the general, collective psychology. Jung believed that each person had a core Self, which was authentic and real. And over the course of life, this Self would either manifest or remain latent, depending on how deeply submerged the individual is in the cultural mythologies of his age. Become too identified with your persona, with your social mask, and your Self will remain hidden to you, or at least you will come to know it much later.

At the same time, he made a clear distinction between individuation and individualism. The process of individuation should not make you more isolated and confined, but more social – to fostering more intense collective relationships. It requires cooperation between the powerful contents of the unconscious and consciousness.

We spend a lot of time trying to realize something, we make plans and arrangements for the future. We have strong impulses for Self-realization. 'Become who you are' is our perennial dictum, but our conscious will, and personal desires cannot alone shape our Self-realization or individual wholeness.

We often try to become what we want to be and not who we are. Here, Jung begins to sound vague and flaky. But the message here is simply that the modern individual is far too invested in their future. They live their lives in a way where they sacrifice the present so that they can reach some future aspiration, to attain this title or that position. In fact, people are so invested in fulfilling this future narrative, that failure to do so would be a total disaster for them psychologically.

Jung thought that social and economic pressures force the individual into this way of thinking, and by falling prey to it, we forego the deeper, more authentic parts of ourselves. Imagine the person who has a deep inclination towards cultivating their garden or working in nature, but the demands of his corporate job in the city do not afford him the time or the luxury of being able to manifest these desires.

"Who we want to be" is an idea that is influenced by ego ideals and aspirations that are not always congruent with our total personality. This may lead to Self-alienation and neurosis. In the second half of life, it is necessary to change our hierarchy of values, according to Jung. Now, what is the risk of not individuating? It is attaching your sense of worth on some external thing. Let us say that our urban dweller who secretly dreams of becoming a gardener is questioned about their highest value. They would say, "money, of course." Jung would object that it is not really money that they are after, but an increase of Self-worth. The more money they attain, the higher their Self-worth. So, in the end, they are appeasing their narcissistic needs.

The problem with centering your ideal on money is the intensive fear that comes with losing it. In the US, after the market crashes of the 1930's and even of the latest crash in 2008, there was an epidemic of suicides. Jung thought that people killed themselves after these events because they literally experienced a loss of Self. And here, we come to the purpose of this digression. Jung's theory of individuation in the end, is just a characterization of the tragic sense of disconnection the individual feels.

Failure to individuate is equivalent to a disconnection from one's core Self, and the manufacturing of false ideals, are ultimately, the construction of instruments that give the individual a temporary feeling of connectedness but are ultimately liable to being destroyed at any point in time. Recall Dustin Hoffman's character in *Death of a Salesman* or the man who loses his wealth after a stock market crash.

There is a story about a businessman, in his fifties, who was so strongly identified with his business that he could not have a conversation without obsessively talking about his company's turnover. As he grew older, he felt the need to expand, and opened more shops. Until then, he had always been a careful, calculating professional. But this clearly changed when he started investing large sums of money on the interior decorating of his shops.

Turnover and profit were no longer the only things that mattered to him – he needed to shift his focus to maintaining an elegant décor. He could explain this change by saying that design was essential for being competitive in the marketplace. But he invested so much money that he wondered if his business would still be profitable, so he phoned the branches each hour to see how sales were going. His mood became dependent on good or bad sales.

Not only was he fearful and emotionally tense, but he experienced fits of rage when sales figures were not up to his expectations. The competent man who managed his sales could not put up with this behavior and decided to leave the company for his competitor.

The businessman then decided to do the job himself and to make sure that things were done properly. But he spent most of his time obsessively standing behind the shop's glass doors waiting for clients. If none or very few clients came, the expression on his face became so gloomy and angry that he must have scared away any potential buyers. He was, in effect, literally standing in the way of his own business interests and the turnover really went down.

He reacted to these real worries by developing high blood pressure and psychosomatic symptoms of all types – which demanded full attention and turned him into a hypochondriac. This behavior gradually became unbearable for himself and others. From that point, nothing could have stopped his business from declining.

The businessman's intensive eagerness to gain Self-importance crushed him. His urge to feel like he was the king of his professional sphere led him to disown everything else in his life. Royal palaces have always been artfully constructed buildings exhibiting great splendor. Buildings devoted to the divine (temples, churches, and cathedrals) have been, since antiquity, designed to exhibit even greater magnificence. They were places where a godhead resides and operates.

It seems that the businessman unconsciously fell prey to this archetypal theme. He wanted a temple for his highest value. But such relentless dedication looks like sacrilege, even in our modern, secularist, capitalist times.

His task was to free himself of this extreme association of his Self-worth to his business – he needed to do some introspection – something that was beyond his abilities. This is not to say that this man should be condemned, for his fate was understandable. The ego fears losing its footing, and this compels it to defensively hold on to certain attitudes.

The Persona

To know the Self, it is necessary to know what it is not. According to Jung, the persona is the false Self that you craft. It is the identity that you have created to blend into groups, and it is how you want others to see you.

Schopenhauer described this function very dearly as "what one appears to oneself and one's surroundings or in the reflection of one's surroundings;" he went on to warn about "the difference between what one is and what one performs." If someone identifies with this role, he should be discriminated against as "personal." His opposite number would be an "individual" person. The expression "personalities" is based on the same phenomenon and is understood as an unpleasant opposite of perfect adaptation, i.e., as egocentricity. or identification with the persona.

- Personality – The Individuation Process, C.A Meier

The persona can be shaped in two different ways:

1. When someone is not aware of his persona, it will appear in his own projection. With the son in a father transference and with a daughter in a mother transference.

2. The second way of remaining unconscious of your persona is by identifying with it. The most common form is with the profession or position one holds.

Thus, Jung identified two ways in which your persona manifests. The first is by unwittingly mimicking the behavior of your same-sex parent. The second is by identifying fully with your profession or social role.

Carl Jung said that the first impediment to individuation is the persona. The individuation process steps require you to:

1. Incorporate your unconscious in a healthy way by recognizing your persona.

2. Integrate your unconscious dreams by analyzing their content.

There is nothing you can do to stop the unconscious from manifesting itself in your conscious reality. You must choose between either letting that manifestation happen destructively or constructively.

It's worth remembering that completing these steps successfully poses a risk to your sanity. A process of individuation that is constructive is desirable, but many will find that to recognize and eliminate your persona is a painful and dangerous task. The second thing you need to do is study your own dreams, which most of us will find very difficult to do without professional help. According to Jung, dreams are the non-repressed plain representations of your unconscious. Untangling that complex mess is a lengthy process that requires patience and skill.

But if you were to start with the first step – you would need to first identify your persona before you can get rid of it – in a healthy way. The persona is usually the role you play either personally or professionally. It is the uniform you wear every day, how you introduce yourSelf to others, and how you carry yourSelf in public.

The persona is the star of a great play that all the other actors are taking part in. Anyone who gets into a career path must adopt a social mask to blend in, to be part of the functional whole. This is because raw individuality is rarely a tenable social strategy.

You learn at a young age that there is an acceptable pattern of behavior that you must manifest. And this will work quite well for you through your adolescent years, and even through early adulthood, but eventually, too strict an identification with the persona will bring about a tragic outcome: you become nothing but persona. It is difficult to know when a persona is doing more harm than good.

Religious traditions, sports teams, political parties, business cultures and any social organization entails a form of blending into the environment. And far from being an optional feature of human beings, there is something essential about social identity. Even if the social identity in question is baseless or dubious to most, there is always a human need to form a social identity where the individual persona is dissolved in the same way that there is an instinct to worship.

Jung, however, understood the dangers that came with social identity and too strong an identification with the persona. You become so attached to your social mask that you have no other sense of Self. Your persona determines what you strive towards, which will determine how you structure your life, which will then determine your future goals. It is as if a vicious circle has been triggered, where your authentic voice gradually gets drowned out.

But this is not catastrophic to other people, since the person who is dominated by their persona can be effective and functional socially and professionally. They can earn money, and the love and admiration of others – they can get anything they want in life and their persona will be instrumental in helping them achieve their goals.

---

*What good will it be for
someone to gain the whole*

world, yet forfeit their soul? Or
what can anyone give in
exchange for their soul?

– Mathew: 16:26

The problem is that if you are nothing but persona, then you are a puppet. You relinquish control completely, and you no longer become the author of your life. If you have no authentic qualities, no connection with your deepest yearnings, and no real Self-knowledge, then you will become wholly pragmatic.

A knife doesn't slice fruit because it wants to eat, similarly, you work and you socialize not because you want to, but because unconscious social forces have compelled you to. You are merely following the whims of the collective.

Imagine a news reporter who is paid to recite a specific narrative every night to millions of people. This person is essentially an actor, and they become fully identified with the message they are delivering, regardless of whether they truly believe it or not.

Usually, they work for a three-lettered broadcasting institution, which has earned a very grandiose reputation over the years. They will sincerely impersonate a phony voice which sounds like no person you have ever seen, except of course, on the news. Curiously, across the generations this static personality keeps its shape, embodying both the male and female forms. This character is capable of smiling, showing outrage and indignation, but ultimately, it is all fake.

They are enacting a parody of themselves, and for these people, or for anyone in any manufactured role in life, it becomes difficult to dissociate from the persona they have crafted. Think of the military officer who carries their authoritarian attitude into their relationships with family and friends. The persona is a tool, it can help you mold into a less ambiguous form, which in turn will make your character more digestible, more familiar, and more likable. But as Jung warns us, brewing in the darkness, in the recesses of your mind is your shadow, it is what is being repressed by your persona.

The persona will not yield encouragement – but will invite harassment, pity, and spite. Those who are honest with themselves will not see you as a beacon of light, but as an obnoxious, ridiculous imitation of a human being. They will not find you memorable or interesting. At best, they will find you amusing. But most often, they will find you irritating.

The persona is not always unsuccessful; indeed, it exists for success and power. It underhandedly attempts its coup when the enemy is least suspecting. It feigns weakness. It is a manifestation of deep, hidden desires for power and social recognition. It is a veteran manipulator of others – and of its owner. It hides in moments of solitude and reappears when the time is right.

But how much persona is it possible to forego without becoming totally alienated from society? This depends on each person and their particular circumstances. That is why, while Jung's insight is useful psychologically, it is not applicable to each person.

Myths

Another important contribution of Jung was highlighting the role of myths in the life of the individual. Of course, he was not alone in making this point. Others, such as Eliade and Campbell have written extensively on this subject.

Jung thought that people repressed their thoughts, which was destructive to their psychology. Neuroses, as Freud taught, were the result of repressed thoughts. But Jung thought that the problem that the modern individual faces is that they are alienated from the myths and rituals of their ancestors. These stories served an important function, they awaken the unconscious ideas that were being repressed. You can bring these ideas to light through being exposed to mythology, you awaken the contents of the unconscious.

Myths imbue our lives with meaning, and they connect us to archetypal ideas that we have a deep, unconscious longing for. But why did Jung believe that myths were so important, and why did he think that they were connected to the conscious?

Through his practice, Jung noticed a peculiar pattern among his patients. When he asked them to draw pictures, they would paint symbols that were thousands of years old, and corresponded to psychological ideas that Jung knew about, but that the patient was not familiar with. The consistency with which this happened suggested that it was highly unlikely that these ideas came from personal experiences, it was more likely that his patients were drawing on stores of information that were much older. Jung thought that each person is in possession of these ideas since birth.

The primitive mentality does not invent myths, it experiences them. Myths are original revelations of the preconscious psyche, involuntary statements about unconscious psychic happenings, and anything but allegories of physical processes.

Such allegories would be an idle amusement for an unscientific intellect. Myths, on the contrary, have a vital meaning. Not merely do they represent, they are the psychic life of the primitive tribe, which immediately falls to pieces and decays when it loses its mythological heritage, like a man who has lost his soul.

– The Archetypes and the Collective Unconscious, Jung

More than that, he believed that knowing your specific ancestry mattered. If you are from Europe, the ideas that you should seek to identify are those of Christianity since it was Christian symbolism that dominated the psyche of your forefathers. While someone from India should seek the symbolism of Hinduism or Buddhism to connect with the archetypal ideas of his ancestors.

According to Nietzsche, the loss of myth is not easily substituted for by science or rationality. Society will seek to restore the remnants of the past; they will struggle to survive without them. An interesting development will occur when myth and science are combined, a topic which we will discuss in the final chapter.

> *Here we have our present age bent on the extermination of myth…. Man today, stripped of myth, stands famished among all his pasts and must dig frantically for roots.*
>
> *– The Birth of Tragedy, Nietzsche*

Thus, individuation is the process by which the individual becomes whole – that is, able to incorporate all the elements of his Self, conscious and unconscious into her life. The archetypal elements that you will find in religious symbolism is a means to connect with the unconscious Self, this is a way to counter our natural inclination towards repression.

The Shadow

> *"Everybody should do in their lifetime two things. One is to consider death, to observe skulls and skeletons, and to wonder what it would be like to go to sleep and never wake up. The other thing to consider is that you are totally Selfish. You*

don't have a good thing to be
said about you at all. You are an
utter rascal."

– Alan Watts

Jung thought that the essential problem, when you do not recognize your capacity for evil, is that you will tend to project it outwards onto others. When people are unaware of their own dark sides, they will inevitably point towards an enemy, and blame them for the evil that exists. Racism and xenophobia find fertile ground in the mind of a person who believes himself to be pure and incorruptible, that under no circumstances, will he resort to cruelty or evil.

If you believe yourSelf to be a good, pure person with no bad intentions – that you are bewildered when you hear of people who are actively trying to destroy everything around them, then you are unaware of your shadow. You have chosen to dissociate form it.

And when you choose to split the shadow, it leads to strange effects. It leads to an undesirable dichotomy – the estrangement of the Self from the Self. The famous story of *The Strange Case of Dr. Jekyll and Mr. Hyde* exemplifies this. Another example of the greater shadow is Nietzsche's Zarathustra. Below are other examples cited by Meier.

> *In Shakespeare, the clearest example of the theme of the "hostile brothers" is probably that of Othello and Iago. and in Goethe it is certainly Faust and Mephistopheles. A very vivid example of what can happen if we allow ourselves to be "taken over" by the shadow can be found in E.T.A. Hoffmann's Brother Medardus in Die Elixiere des Teufeis (1814). In Carl Spitteler's early work Prometheus and Epimetheus, a Parable (1881). Prometheus, as an introvert, clearly represents the soul and Epimetheus. as an extrovert, represents the world. The "ugliest person" in Nietzsche's Zarathustra is certainly a classic example of the unreflected shadow.*
>
> *Personality: The Individuation Process. C.A. Meier*

Usually, hero myths show the overcoming of the opposite member, and the result is that the ego grows into the universally human. The problem of the shadow is important because its conscious processing is critical to the conflict with the unconscious. In the story of Jekyll and Hyde, Jekyll writes a letter where he reveals his situation.

Jekyll starts by introducing us to his background – he comes from a wealthy family, is endowed with good health, and inclined by nature to industry. He is fond of wisdom and does good among his fellowmen – he has everything going for him. His only fault is his impatient cheerfulness, but he has found it difficult to reconcile this drive with his desire to carry his head high.

Hence it came about that I concealed my pleasures; and that when I reached years of reflection, and began to look round me and take stock of my progress and position in the world, I stood already committed to a profound duplicity of me.

The Strange Case of Dr Jekyll and Mr. Hyde, Robert Louis Stevenson

---

Many people irreverently express these pleasures, but because of Jekyll's high ideals, he viewed them with a morbid sense of shame. It was the unrealistic nature of his expectations, rather than his faults that made him what he was – he had severed his connection with his opposite, hidden Self. He did not think of himself as a hypocrite, his conflicting sides were sincere and earnest. He felt more himself when he was either.

And it chanced that the direction of my scientific studies, which led wholly towards the mystic and the transcendental, reacted and shed a strong light on this consciousness of the perennial war among my members. With every day, and from both sides of my intelligence, the moral and the intellectual, I thus drew steadily nearer to that truth, by whose partial discovery I have been doomed to such a dreadful shipwreck: that man is not truly one, but truly two.

The Strange Case of Dr Jekyll and Mr. Hyde, Robert Louis Stevenson

He marched in one direction, the congruous proper path. He recognized through himself, the primitive duality of man.

Dr. Jekyll figured out how to create a potion to grant him this wish – to transform into the ugly side of his nature, without remorse, and without damaging his own reputation. He reasoned that if each side could do what it wanted, he would be relieved of all torment, and would be delivered from the remorse of his upright nature – that his evil Self could march forward confidently, doing whatever gave it pleasure.

Creativity plays an important role in individuation. A creative lifestyle allows the individual to confront his problems on his own and to express himself in finding creative solutions. This gives him a sense of Self-reliance, and the courage he needs to be creative. It also gives him Self-esteem, a feeling which modern people badly need to avoid being lost in the masses.

The Folly of Pride

An archetype is a timeless representation of inevitable patterns of human behavior. We will always have wise sages, warriors, and tricksters. In *The Hero with a Thousand Faces,* Joseph Campbell identifies the main archetypes and shows us how they are represented in different cultures through myths and stories.

To Jung, archetypes were, and still are, living psychic forces that demand to be taken seriously. They are the unfailing causes of neurotic and psychotic disorders. behaving like neglected or maltreated physical organs.

"Pride is ugly in all men, it is worse than cruelty, which is the worst of sins, and humility is better than clemency, which is the best of good deeds."

– Al-Jahiz

Jung thought that when you become aware of your ignorance, capacity for evil, tendency to repress subconscious states of the Self, you begin to work to remedy your own flaws. Further, you easily recognize such flaws in other people who might possess the charm, charisma, and wit to coerce others into following their lead. By rejecting pride, you refuse to accept the flawed aspects of yourSelf that are within your control.

It is a most painful procedure to tear off those veils, but each step forward in psychological development means just that, the tearing off of a new veil. We are like onions with many skins, and we have to peel ourselves again and again in order to get at the real core."

The integration of your shadow requires you to reject pride and your persona. It requires you to accept the reality of your nature – with its flaws, and construct a Self-image that is far from idealistic, but unique, realistic, and authentic. But what is individuation? And when do we know we are done?

Jung never set a deadline. He believed that the process of individuation never ends. It is a lifelong mission where we are always trying to acknowledge our inferior and hidden sides, whether it is the persona, the shadow, or anima/animus.

Archetypes are relatively autonomous – they have their own objectives. It is not possible to integrate them through rational methods. A dialectical procedure is required.

That is one way the individuation process could be accelerated. Jung described it as a conversation with one's good angel. Another way to accelerate this individuation process is to study your dreams. By recording your dreams and studying their contents over a long period of time, you are making yourSelf more aware of the realm of the unconscious and the images and content that it contains.

"That passion is better than stoicism or hypocrisy; that straightforwardness, even in evil, is better than losing oneself in trying to observe traditional morality; that the free man is just as able to be good as evil, but that the unemancipated man is a disgrace to nature, and has no share in heavenly or earthly bliss ; finally, that all who wish to be free must become so through themselves, and that freedom falls to nobody's lot as a gift from Heaven."

Richard Wagner in Bayreuth, Nietzsche Vol. I. of this Translation, pp. 199-200

Since the instinctivist tradition began with Darwin, let us first briefly look at what Darwin had to say, before moving on to Marx, Freud, and Lorenz.

Darwin lived in the dawn of the industrial revolution, in a world totally transformed. Before the Enlightenment, Europe existed in a primitive state – no steam engine, no trains, no cars, no machines. Life was slow, and people were tougher. Since sedatives hadn't been developed, people's threshold for pain was much higher. And science was a strange, esoteric pastime that a minority of people engaged in, usually aristocrats.

In *The Discovery of the Unconscious*, Ellenberger takes us through a journey to this pivotal era, where we learn about the intellectual development of Europe.

A History of Environments

Dichotomy 15: Nature vs Nurture

There is a good chance that at some point in your life, you have heard the terms "nature versus nurture." The proponents for the "nature" side of the debate or the instinctivists (Freud and Lorenz). Even Jung can be considered an instinctivist.

In direct opposition are the environmentalists – the "nurture" proponents. To this group, man's behavior is totally molded by the influence of the environment (social, cultural) rather than innate factors. In particular, this is true for aggression, a large obstacle in the way of progress.

The philosophers of the Enlightenment presented the radical version of this view by claiming that man was born "good" and rational, and it was only because of the corrupting influences of society that he develops evil desires.

Some refused any physical differences between the sexes and suggested that any differences, other than anatomical ones, came from education and tradition. In contrast to behaviorism, these thinkers did not care about methods of human engineering and manipulation. They were advocates of social and political change. They believed that a reformed society would create a "good" man, or simply, would allow the naturally good man to remain uncorrupted. Rousseau comes to mind.

Jean-Jacques Rousseau was an 18th century Genevan philosopher, writer, and composer. His work preceded the psychoanalysts. Rousseau experienced his first literary success later in life. The Academy of Dijon offered a prize for the best essay on the question: Have the arts and sciences conferred benefits on mankind?

In his essay, Rousseau maintained the negative and won the prize (1750).

He argued that science, letters, and the arts are the worst enemies of morals, and, by creating wants, are the sources of slavery; for how can chains be imposed on those who go naked, like American savages? As might be expected, he is for Sparta, and against Athens.

Like the Spartans, he took success in war as the test of merit, but he admired the 'noble savage', whom sophisticated Europeans could defeat in war. He thought that science and virtue are incompatible, and all sciences have an ignoble origin and that astronomy comes from the superstition of astrology; eloquence from ambition; geometry from avarice; physics from vain curiosity; and even ethics has its source in human pride. Education and the art of printing are to be deplored; everything that distinguishes civilized man from the untutored barbarian is evil.

Having won the prize and achieved sudden fame by this essay, Rousseau took to living according to its maxims. He adopted the simple life, and sold his watch, saying that he would no longer need to know the time.

Rousseau believed that man, in his natural form, was good. And that it was society that imprinted amoral behavior on the individual. Get rid of civilizing forces, and you get rid of amorality.

Behaviorism

John B. Watson (1878-1958)

In 1913, behaviorism was founded by J.B. Watson; it was based on the idea that "the subject matter of human psychology is the behavior or activities of the human being. " Anything that could not be directly observed (desire, sensation, perception, emotion, thoughts) were discounted. The underlying idea of behaviorism was that human beings were products of their environment. Like Rousseau, the environmentalist believed that the individual's ethics and behavior were a by-product of environmental influences. Want to change human thought and action? Change the environment.

B.F Skinner

Behaviorism went through remarkable changes. From the unsophisticated formulations of Watson to the genius of Skinner. But this development never saw further depth or originality, but mainly a refinement of the original thesis. B.F Skinner's brand of neobehaviorism, like Watson's behaviorism, rejected any phenomena that could not be observed.

The new psychology-as-a-science approach advanced by Skinner refused to entertain fuzzy concepts like goals or intentions, remnants of a pre-scientific era. Skinner thought that psychology should study the reinforcements that shape human behavior and learn how to apply these reinforcements most effectively. Skinner's psychology was the science of behavioral engineering. It had one aim. Find the right triggers to produce the desired behavior.

Pavlov, a Russian physiologist, introduced classical conditioning. Pavlov showed that when a bell was sounded each time the dog was fed, the dog learned to associate the sound with the presentation of the food. Skinner went beyond this. He introduced "operant" conditioning. That is, unconditioned behavior, if it is desirable from the experimenter's perspective, is rewarded (or followed by pleasure).

Skinner thought that rewards were more effective than punishments. The subject will eventually come to behave in the desire fashion. For example, if a child hates broccoli, his mother can reward him with a piece of candy every time he ate the dreaded green vegetable. Over time, the child would come to associate broccoli with pleasurable candy and will develop healthy eating habits (minus the candy presumably).

Skinner showed, through hundreds of experiments how operant conditioning worked. With the proper use of positive reinforcement, animals and humans can be trained to go against many of their "innate" tendencies.

The moral issue with Skinner's experiments is that they are not so much designed with a goal or end. The purpose of the experiments is to prove that subjects can be manipulated, while the experimenters try to discover the most effective ways to manipulate their subjects. Like any powerful technology, you can see how this can go wrong.

Skinner's extraordinary popularity can be explained by the fact that he has succeeded in blending elements of traditional, optimistic, liberal thought with the social and mental reality of cybernetic society. Skinner believes that man is malleable, subject to social influences, and that nothing in his nature" can be

considered to be a final obstacle
to development toward a
peaceful and just society.

– The Anatomy of Human
Destructiveness, Erich Fromm

Skinner's system appeals to any scientist who is liberal in orientation and is optimistic about society's ability to attain ideals like peace and equality. The design of a better society on scientific principles is an endeavor that Fromm compares to Marxism.

Yet, the "liberal" society that escaped Marxism is not so liberal. And it may be this fact that has allowed behaviorism to thrive.

In the cybernetic age, the individual becomes increasingly subject to manipulation, Fromm writes. Everything he does – his work, consumption, and leisure are manipulated by advertising and ideologies (what Skinner calls "positive reinforcements." The individual loses his active and responsible role in the social world, and he becomes totally "adjusted." He learns that if he does behave according to the general scheme, then he will be at a severe disadvantage, and that he is what he is supposed to be.

When I discussed Freud's ideas, I mentioned the conflict between the individual and civilization. With the advent of behaviorism, this conflict was magnified. The individual is no longer at odds with civilizing forces, but his very nature – his thoughts, beliefs, and actions – are manipulated by them. And this is not done in an Orwellian form of a boot stepping down on the throat of man for all eternity, but in a much more subtle way. Aldous Huxley or Phillip K. Dick had a better idea when they imagined the future. The insidious thing was that the individual would no longer be able to tell the difference between freedom and unfreedom.

If the individual holds onto his individuality, he risks his freedom or his life (in some police states), and in some democracies, he risks losing his job, or being demoted. He also risks feeling isolated.

Most people are not clearly aware of their discomfort.

> *Skinner recommends the hell of the isolated, manipulated man of the cybernetic age as the heaven of progress. He dulls our fears of where we are going by telling us that we need not be afraid; that the direction our industrial system has taken is the same as that which the great humanists had dreamt of, except that it is scientifically grounded.*

*– The Anatomy of Human
Destructiveness, Erich Fromm*

Skinner's theory rings true because it is mostly true for the modern individual, who at best, can feel empowered by the idea that the system he finds himself in is in the end designed with his best interest in mind. '

In the 1920's, psychology's focus shifted from feeling to behavior. Emotions and passion became irrelevant. This culminated in neobehaviorism, which is still popular today.

Neobehaviorism

Neobehaviorism adds a couple of twists to the behaviorist framework. First, neobehaviorism shifts the focus from overt organismic behavior to the underlying neurological drivers of behavior.

In *The Hacking of the American Mind*, Robert Lustig argues that all human behaviors are manifestations of the biochemistry that drives them. In other words, we behave the way we do because of processes happening in our brain. A study by Olds and Milner showed that rats with electrodes in their brain would press a lever to Self-administer shocks more than 7500 times over 12 hours.

This majestic response rate pushed the authors to hypothesize that they had found a system within the brain whose specific function was to produce a rewarding effect on behavior. The reinforcer in this case was not an external source of nourishment, like food pellets, but an internal entity originating in the brain's pleasure centers.

Neobehaviorists focus on the neurotransmitter dopamine, which is rumored to create an intense feeling of pleasure when released in the brain. Thus, dopamine acts like a powerful reinforcement that drives our behavior, including frequent technology use. A like on Instagram or Facebook apparently triggers a burst of dopamine in the brain, which is why it feels so good. Over time, these intermittent feelings of pleasure set up an operant conditioning that compels us to come back for more. Classical conditioning involves associating an involuntary response and a stimulus, while operant conditioning is about associating a voluntary behavior and a consequence.

The second twist is that neobehaviorists replaced the behaviorist concept of operant conditioning with the psychopathological concept of addiction. For example, frequent technological use is not just a learned behavior or a habit but is a behavioral addiction. This is problematic, of course, because it is not technological fasts that ought to be recommended as remedies for adults and children, but total abstinence. Unless, of course, we are also okay with telling children to just lay off the heroin for a little while. In any case, as the author Jesper Aagaard argued, the main shortcoming of neurobehaviorism is not its inconsistency but its pathological rhetoric, which frames addiction as a problem afflicting the general population.

Chapter 3: The Dichotomy of the Fool and the Narcissist

Psychoanalysis: Science or Hoax?

The Elusive Mind

During the end of the 16th century, there was the birth of modern science. Knowledge before this point depended on deduction and observation, while modern scientific knowledge is based on experimentation and measurement. Science aims to unify human knowledge. There is only one science, which has many branches. This means that distinct schools cannot exist side by side, each with its own methodology. Medicine thus became a branch of science, and psychiatry a branch of medicine, and psychotherapy an application of psychiatry – based on scientific conclusions.

In that sense, the physician becomes more a technician and specialist. Since science is all-inclusive knowledge, it cannot admit that extra scientific healing has any validity, and this explains the contempt of "official" medicine for all other kinds of medicine, including primitive and popular medicine (which contains elements of primitive medicine).

But modern dynamic psychiatry is divided into several "schools" as we have seen. Does this mean dynamic psychotherapy is a regression into the past, or rather that the scientific method was unable to cover the total personality of man, and must be replaced by other approaches?

Most people fall into one of two camps. They take psychoanalytic ideas very seriously or they think that they are a joke. Those who take it seriously do so for various reasons. Either they have personally profited from it, or they have found truth in the ideas of psychoanalysts like Freud, Jung, Adler, Klein, Kohut, Rank, Lacan. And those who do not take it seriously, refer to thinkers like Popper who quickly demonstrated the flaw with unfalsifiable science (such as psychoanalysis), and they turn to events the failure of psychological studies to replicate (50 percent). Or they compare the failings of psychology with the splendor of the hard sciences, often oblivious to the fact that the latter has undergone several paradigm shifts in the past few centuries.

There is no question that the effectiveness of the hard sciences, and the predictability and dependability of its discoveries are far closer to an objective account of reality, if such an account exists. But there is a mistaken tendency to worship the hard sciences, precisely for this incredible power that has endowed the human being.

But we should remember that while the workings of the human mind cannot be known through laboratory investigations, as Jung intuited, the natural scientists are constantly bewildered by their attempts to explain the physical reality.

Only recently have we discovered the pathology of too much hygiene, and the importance of good gut bacteria. Only recently have we discovered the important role that fat plays in weight reduction. Only recently have we discovered the importance of breathing through the nose, or chewing hard objects, or the benefits of fasting.

The irony is that you can find more similar patterns in highly speculative psychoanalytic ideas, when you zoom out, than you can in diet recommendations based on the nutritional sciences.

The more scientists try to untangle the mysteries of the universe, the more they find themselves struggling with even more mysteries. That is not a critique against science, but an acknowledgement of the inherent complexity that exists in the universe, and our limited abilities to understand any of it. And so, when we frame the picture in this way, we can forgive the psychoanalysts for failing to tell us how the world's most mysterious organ works, in a consistent, coherent, and predictive way.

But aside from the two camps, the believers in psychoanalysis or psychology and the unbelievers, there is a third camp, and this is the camp I find most interesting. This is a group of people who see the impact that psychology has had on culture and society. They see how advertising, for example, is an enterprise that is built on our understanding of the unconscious. Edward Bernayes, Freud's nephew, contributed to various commercials and ideas that elevated advertising into a new age.

Today, there are people like Martin Lindstrom who are advertising superstars, and they make their money by giving companies insights into people's unconscious. And then you have Silicon Valley, an entire industry devoted to created apps and games that are based on the principles of behaviorism and neobehaviorism.

Finally, as commentators such as Lasch and Rieff have pointed out, there is the intellectual legacy left behind by Freud, it is one that has to do with how people think, how they view their relationship with God and the cosmos and with themselves. The psychologizing away of the concept of God created an existential vacuum that is currently filled with a remix of incoherent religious beliefs mixed with new age fluff. In addition, there is the rise of transhumanism, a technological movement, or a techno religion, Kastrup called it singularism, that aims to mold man in the image of God.

In the *Age of Spiritual Machines* Kurzweil says that it doesn't really matter what we want, that the future is inevitably moving in this direction, towards the singularity at an ever-increasing pace. The only choice left for us is to either embrace it and accept it or join the luddites and become ostracized from society.

This echoes the ideas of a French Catholic philosopher, Jacques Eliul, who advanced the idea that technique will continue to improve upon itself independent of human wellbeing. Like Freud's primordial drives, Eros and Thanatos, technique is not interested in human happiness, prosperity, or wellbeing, but merely the evolution of itself.

There are many ideas that accurately describe a part of the human experience, but there will always be something left over, something for which we have no explanation for. And we must never content ourselves with ignorance, even if we knew that perfect knowledge is an impossible goal. It is usually the mark of the obsessive and unrealistic person to demand a final truth for anything, not least of which the human mind. It is hard enough to know if the external world, which is far more transparent to us, is moving in the right direction.

When our expectations are so high, we abandon the adventure altogether, convinced that we will never reach the pinnacle that we have set in our sights. But if we have learned anything from our collective human experience, it is that true progress occurs through incremental steps.

There are a few things we can take away from the discussion of various psychological ideas so far.

First, among these many ideas are interesting commentaries on the human condition, but they are merely interpretations or points of view. While they contain elements of truth, they are not necessarily true.

That is, they are not more profound or insightful about human nature, than a great philosophy or novel – which is not to say that they lack insight. Psychoanalytic theories offer a perspective on human nature that can be illuminating, but equally, it can be misleading. And very little of these ideas are scientifically proven. We may have an intuition to accept them or not, but this has more to do with us than with the ideas.

Second, there are many contradictions between the psychologists themselves. There are many things that Jung disagrees with Freud about, or that Adler disagrees with Freud and Jung about. And these are foundational ideas, not trivial points. So, the early psychoanalytic schools are more like the philosophical schools that argued with one another in ancient Greece, that they are to the "hard" forms of science such as physics or chemistry.

Having said that, it is important to remember that even the hard sciences experience radical shifts in paradigms over time. At any given point in time, the scientific consensus is almost certainly wrong. And as Kuhn notes, it is not as if new theories necessarily build on old theories, but in many cases, replace the old theories altogether. So, one feature, not merely of psychoanalysis, but of all forms of human knowledge, in general, is that it is very likely incomplete, mistaken, or confused.

Third, recall the importance of Romanticism on the development of the ideas of Freud and Jung. And recall the "unmasking" trend which defined the era they lived in. Very little of what Freud and Jung discovered was truly original. Their theories were in the end, a mixing of mashing of various schools of thought, philosophies, cultural and technological trends at the time.

All of this to say that when reading about psychoanalytical ideas, one must not merely consume these ideas with a "pinch" of salt, but should keep in mind, that in addition to salt, there are numerous other spices that have been added to the dish, and many of these spices are unknown or unfamiliar to us – thus, contributing to the sense of mystery and bewilderment that we sense in these ideas.

The mistake here, would be to turn our back on the psychoanalytical ideas and presume that a better reading of human nature can be achieved in the laboratory.

The Replication Crisis

To what extent can experiments in a laboratory inform us about the human mind? The replication crisis in the social sciences suggest the answer is "to some extent" but not much more.

Brian Nosek estimated the reproducibility of 100 studies in psychological science from three high-ranking psychology journals.[40] Overall, 36% of the replications yielded significant findings (p value below 0.05) compared to 97% of the original studies that had significant effects. ii

According to an article by *The Atlantic*, a different attempt to replicate findings from psychology failed half the time, some of these studies include the ideas of social priming (subliminal messages affect behavior), ego depletion (our will power is limited and can run out), and facial feedback (forcing ourselves to smile makes us feel happier).

Why the poor results? It could be because researchers choose to hide away negative results. Whenever their experiment fails to corroborate their hypothesis, they may simply choose to hide it away from sight. Another thing they do is "p-hacking" – they play with the variables of their study so that it ends up fitting an acceptable confidence interval (for example, 5 percent).

In 2005, the epidemiologist John Ioannidis explained the problematic nature of scientific research. He argued that much of scientific research was undermined by the base rate fallacy. He wrote a paper about it called *Why Most Published Research Findings Are False*.

There may be other simple explanations to why this crisis exists, including incompetent researchers – but the problem of gaining insight into the human mind through lab experiments is a very old one.

In *The Discovery of the Unconscious*, Ellenberger mentions a story about one of the pioneers of psychoanalysis, whose ideas I have discussed in this book, Carl Jung.

Jung repeated a word association test for years that he thought would help detect criminals, but he abandoned the test when he realized that it was much more complicated. Jung eventually proclaimed that "whatsoever wishes to know about the human mind will learn nothing, or almost nothing, from experimental psychology."

Unlike Adler or Janet, who were more concerned with knowledge derived from clinical expertise, Jung belonged to the Romantic tradition, he believed people were driven by collective unconscious ideas that were much deeper than human rationality, and that there was a powerful need for people to subscribe to these archetypal modes of thinking and enact them through their behavior.

One-Dimensional Man

One of the interesting observations of Marcuse's *One-Dimensional Man* (written in 1964) is that society's rejection of the irrational and embrace of the rational has resulted in a paradoxical outcome: a small portion of society that is hyper-rational, while the rest have become increasingly irrational.

Modern rationality has become so advanced that the newest innovation in science have become completely inaccessible to most people. One scientist, in the documentary, *Technocalyps*, remarked that it would take around 50 years for an intelligent person to get up to speed with modern mathematics. The line between wizardry and technological innovation is becoming increasingly thinner. And perhaps, for that reason, the technologists of Silicon Valley are no longer seen merely as captains of industry, but the new religious and spiritual leaders.

The insight we get, not just from psychology, but by observing human behavior throughout history, is that people must worship something. Anything. If not supernatural God(s), scripture, and holy prophets, then something else.

If someone is more sensitive, perhaps they worship a guru who promises them serenity and calm in the present moment. And if one is aggressive (or repressive), they worship a totalitarian dictator. If they are cerebral, they may worship the gods of innovation, the techno-utopians that promise them divinity, or the gods of finance, that promise them heaven on earth, or the gods of science and philosophy, that promise them an unbiased understanding of the nature of all things. If they are remarkably shallow and vain, they may worship the celebrities of hyper-reality (or Instagram), that promise them validation and status.

Whatever the nature of the emptiness that exists within everyone that pushes them to worship, I cannot comment on. It only is apparent that it exists. There are those who will pontificate about the root of worship, perhaps like Freud, psychologizing it away to some hidden incestuous or patricidal urge. And there is the Nietzschean intuition that such an instinct exists, and that is not the same as attention. Worship, unlike attention, is unconscious. You choose what you want to give your attention to. You don't choose what you want to worship. And for that reason, it is more mysterious.

Nietzsche, long before the advent of psychotherapy, understood the primacy of the religious instinct. He invented Zarathustra, a Zoroastrian prophet, who came to preach the doctrine of no divinity, in Biblical style (a parable).

Your Self laughs at your Ego and its proud leapings. 'What are these leapings and flights of thought to me?' it says to itself. 'A by-way to my goal. I am the Ego's leading-string and I prompt its conceptions.'

I want to say a word to the despisers of the body. It is their esteem that produces this disesteem. What is it that created esteem and disesteem and value and will?

The creative Self created for itself esteem and disesteem, it created for itself joy and sorrow. The creative body created spirit for itself, as a hand of its will.

Even in your folly and contempt, you despisers of the body, you serve your Self. I tell you: your Self itself wants to die and turn away from life.

Thus Spoke Zarathustra, Nietzsche

The Self that is described by Nietzsche is the unconscious that Freud and Jung acknowledged. But the key difference is that

Nietzsche says that this unconscious is unknowable. It is like scientific knowledge, no matter how much further you advance your knowledge, you will never reach an upper limit. The Self directs, but the Self is not conscious, and not knowable – unlike attention, which can be directed and controlled.

Freud famously psychoanalyzed away the idea of God, but his disciples, Jung and Adler, went on to establish their own pseudo-religions, as detailed in *The Triumph of the Therapeutic* by Rieff. Freud's disciples couldn't accept that the answer to man's existential angst was to worship "nothing." Even more, they could not accept that the answer was to worship science, in its ideological extreme (scientism) like Freud. Jung wanted to establish that man had an innate religious nature, but that the transcendence of his ideas lay not in a divine authority, but in the collective unconscious. Like the Nones today, Jung was not willing to call himself a total atheist.

If man must worship something, then what?

The Self is a poor candidate, since too much Self-love can lead to megalomania and delusional ideas (Secondary Narcissism). Even if one were to abandon Freud's ideas of narcissism (they are debatable) one can easily see the trappings of unregulated Self-concern. The irony is that psychotherapy itself, with its call to search for answers within yourSelf, may be a part of the problem that it is trying to help solve.

In the culture of the therapeutic, people become convinced that the cure to their problems is Self-understanding. They debilitate themselves further, by seeking to gain an understanding of a "Self" that is unknowable.

Protestantism is, perhaps, the ultimate religion of the printed book. The Remixed religions we're about to explore are the religions of the Internet.

Strange Rites: New Religions for a Godless World, Tara Isabella Burton

---

A remixed religion occurs when people choose to blend two or more belief systems with each other, by carefully (or not so carefully) selecting whichever parts of each religion they find convenient. For example, many people have isolated meditation from the practice of Buddhism. Today, meditation is a global phenomenon, and companies are promoting it as a productivity tool. Ironic, since the entire purpose of meditation is detachment from early and material desires.

The internet, with its limitless access to information, burdens the individual with not merely being aware that so many different points of view exist, but integrating as many points as they can to their own belief system.

Thus, to understand why the modern world has so many cults, mixed religions, and new forms of meaning emerging so frequently, we need to look at not only the history of religious belief, but the history of madness.

Rieff wrote that one of the features of the modern world is that everyone is somehow broken. If they are not being as "effective" as they can be, or capable of "relating to others" well enough, or buying into social fictions willingly, then they are "sick." The reality may be that they are not docile enough to be considered normal.

In *The Myth of Mental Illness*, the main point that Szasz makes is that psychological diseases keep changing over time. Szasz recalled that not long ago, there were less than twenty psychological illnesses – then, during his lifetime there were hundreds. It is not that change itself is indicative of foul play – without change, there is no evolution or advancement, but the problem is that we have not really discovered new illnesses, as much as we have re-categorized old behaviors. In any case, the role of the therapist is essentially to socialize the individual into the normal functions of society.

But this is not so much a criticism as much as it is a widely accepted observation. To the criticism launched by Szasz, the modern psychiatrist would nod in agreement, and happily acknowledge that their objective is to socialize the individual into the normal functions of society. Why do Szasz and Foucault (in *Madness and Civilization*) see the need to make a criticism that the psychological establishment would happily concede to?

It has something to do with how the mad used to be treated.

> *There was a time when the mad were mobile, when they interacted with society, and people heard them speak.*
>
> *— Miguel de Cervantes Saavedra, Don Quixote*

In the past, some societies looked for divine wisdom by consulting the mad. Divine madness, also known as theia mania and crazy wisdom, refers to unconventional, outrageous, unexpected, or unpredictable behavior linked to religious or spiritual pursuits. Examples of divine madness can be found in Hellenism,

Christianity, Hinduism, Buddhism, Sufism, and Shamanism.

Divine Madness

Foucault, in *Madness and Civilization*, reminds the reader that there was a time when to be mad meant to be unproductive, thus the vagabonds, the idle, and the youth who had squandered the family fortune were labelled as mad.

But over time, society's perspective on the mad shifted. Madness became a threat. One remedy to curing the mad was in throwing cold water at them. But in the end, confinement emerged as the most practical solution.

Madness was finally recognized as non-reason, or the negation of reason – that is, non-being – insofar as it is cut off from external stimuli. In fact, doctors prescribed travel and ocean waves to restore movement, and thus the correct flow of thoughts in the mind. To cure madness, by language, for example, was to follow the madman in their illusion, or to force them to come out of their condition out of necessity (the need to work and survive).

Eventually, the mad were no longer allowed to be mobile and were locked up in prisons to make sure they were productive and not just a drag on society, they were forced to work. Ironically, this had the effect of displacing "normal" people in society from jobs, and then those people were labelled as "mad", and the cycle continued.

Then in the 19th century, it was only the unproductive mad people that were considered "mad" – this marked the beginning of the asylum.

They were forced to work so that they did not violate one of God's commandments. The work was a way to fix their soul, and consequently, absolve them of guilt. But that was not the only rationale. There was an idea that work was a way to cure man from his suffering.

When man escapes the law of labor that nature imposes on him, he seeks a world of anti-nature, and artifice, and his madness becomes only one manifestation of such a world. In describing how he succeeded, by industrious activity in being cured, Bernadin de-Saint Pierre said:

It was to Jean-Jacques Rousseau that I owed my return to health. I had read, in his immortal writings, among other natural truths, that man is made to work, not to meditate. Until that time I had exercised my soul and rested my body; I changed my ways; I exercised my body and rested my soul. I gave up most books; I turned my eyes to the works of nature,

which addressed all my senses
in a language that neither time
nor nations can corrupt.

Madness and Civilization,
Foucault

The next stage, psychiatry, is when the analyst takes the role of the priest. The patient, or the madman, confesses to them their sins. In a sense, the madman is like a child while the analyst/therapist is the adult. Merely by virtue of rationality vs non-rationality, the therapist had the upper hand and did not need to use any physical force.

That was Foucault's contention against Freud, that one did not need to archive mountains of data on a patient to analyze them. it was sufficient to merely be the rational person in the room, and in that sense, you could hold up a mirror to the madman or the patient, and they would be able to see the errors in their thinking for themselves. This contrasts with Jung, who preferred not to maintain this hierarchical relationship.

There are two points of criticism here. One, the very definition of madness is dubious, not only because it keeps changing with time to reclassify old modes of behavior, but because there are political and financial incentives to convince people that they are dysfunctional.

Second, the therapist has merely filled the void that was previously occupied by the priest, the family, and traditional institutions, and this is the thesis advanced by Rieff and Lasch.

Psychology faces one final limitation: the subject-subject problem. That is, the scientific study of subjective experience requires a subject to be an objective observer of subjective experiences. On the one hand, it is impossible to derive an ought from an is. You cannot falsify psychological ideas.

Primitive Healing

Therefore, as scientific hypotheses, psychological ideas (Adler, Freud, Jung) fail. In any case, most of their ideas were contradicted by the later psychologists (Horney, Kohut, Klein). But that would be the wrong lens to view these ideas. A better approach would be to see the ideas of psychoanalysis as a philosophy, like Epicureanism or Stoicism, no less valuable and important to the human experience, which we will get to in a moment.

The origins of dynamic psychotherapy can be traced back to primitive peoples (medicine men, shamans). While to civilized people, the sight of a medicine man extracting an illness appears to be nonsensical quackery, it is important to understand that these methods were often effective. It is impossible to understand the meaning of this belief or custom without taking into consideration the sociological nature of the community.

There are many accounts of demonic possession in the Western world over the last twenty centuries. But the manifestation of possession and stories of with-hunting gradually disappeared, mostly because of the influence of the Enlightenment, which dispelled belief in the devil – even religious circles gave less importance to him.

But there are other ways in which rudimentary forms of psychotherapy was used. People often feel that their lives were dull and uninteresting, and received no attention from their fellow men, including their families. There are accounts from Madagascar, for example, that show that therapeutic procedures were aimed directly towards the gratification of these frustrated needs.

Primitive healers played a more essential role in his community than the modern physician.

> Sigerist writes: "It is an insult to the medicine man to call him the ancestor of the modern physician. He is that, to be sure, but he is much more, namely the ancestor of most of our professions."

*He is not only concerned with
the welfare of his people (from
making rain to providing victory
in war); he is often a dreaded
wizard, is sometimes the bard
who knows of the origin of the
world and of the history of his
tribe.*

*The Discovery of the
Unconscious, Ellenberger*

One remarkable feature of archaic Eastern cultures was the elaboration of highly developed techniques of mental training, often with psychotherapeutic results, founded on philosophical and religious ideas. Most famous among them is Yoga, a highly elaborated mystical technique.

In the West, techniques of mental training are associated with philosophical schools. In the Greco-Roman era, the practice of philosophy was not merely the acceptance of a doctrine. The Pythagoreans, the Platonists, the Aristotelians, the Stoics, and the Epicureans were not just adherents to philosophical ideas, but members of organized schools called "sects" that imposed on them a specific method of training and a way of life. Each school practices and taught a method of psychic training.

The Pythagoreans, a community bound by strict discipline, followed severe dietary restrictions, exercises in Self-control and in memory recall. They studied mathematics, astronomy, and music.

The Platonists searched for truth, which was expected to be a by-product of the conversations between teachers and students.

The Aristotelian school was a research institute of encyclopedic scope. The idea of psychic training was stressed among the Stoics and Epicureans. The Stoics learned to control emotions and practiced written and verbal exercises in meditation and concentration. They chose a topic – for example, death – and the goal was to dissociate it from all established opinions, fears, and memories that are associated with it. Another practice was "consolations" which were written or told to a person in sorrow.

The Epicureans avoided facing evil directly, they evoked past and future joys. They resorted to an intensive memorization of maxims, which they constantly recited either mentally or out loud. These actions undoubtedly exerted psychotherapeutic action in many individuals.

Some think that Stoicism has certain features that can be found in the Adlerian and existentialist schools of today, and that some of the characteristics of Plato's Academy can be found in the Jungian school, whereas Epicurus tried to remove anxiety, and in that sense, has been compared to Freud.

Philosophical psychotherapy did not merely consist of the methods of collective education. discipline, and mental training that they taught on a collective level. They could also inspire methods for individual therapy, as evidenced by Galen's treatise On the Passions of the Soul.

The Discovery of the Unconscious, Ellenberger

Dichotomy 16: Ontological Security vs Ontological Insecurity

The *Divided Self* by R. D Laing is a landmark book in psychology that made a lasting impact on psychiatry. Since it was published in 1960, much of the book's content applies to a different time, but some of the ideas are far more permanent – in particular, Laing's dichotomy between ontological security and insecurity.

Laing criticized the psychological establishment because psychiatrists were neither humane nor intelligent in the way they interacted with psychotic patients. Instead of seeing them as people who had access to a different kind of experience than they did, psychotics were stigmatized and misunderstood and rather arrogantly by psychiatrists who were quick to put on labels on them. Going back to McGilchrist's left-brain vs right-brain dichotomy – psychiatrists were emphatically left-brained, studying their patients as if they were machines. They understood the outside behaviors but made no effort to see things from the perspective of psychotics.

That is where Laing excelled. He decided to listen to what schizophrenic and schizoid patients told him, and to see things from their point of view. There is an important distinction to be drawn. A schizoid and a schizophrenic both experience a split, either in their own minds, or between themselves and the outside world – according to Laing. They experience an irreconcilable separation. They thus feel like they lack a coherent and stable Self, and to the extent that they do feel that they are integrated, they experience a disconnect with the outside world. Their life is a constant battle against human beings who they think want to change their behavior.

But the schizoid figured out how to adapt while the schizophrenic goes into psychosis.

The primary distinction that Laing makes between these kinds of patients and the "normal" individual is something he called "ontological security." The reason why these dichotomies (within the Self, or between the Self and the world) are drawn up by the patients is because of a lack of ontological security. Most people go through life taking or granted their own sense of identity. They feel as if they have a relatively stable Self with secure foundations. They can enter relationships with other people without fearing that their character and personality or sense of Self would become changed in some irreparable way. Most people feel a sense of ontological security.

But schizoids and schizophrenics lack this basic sense of security. To them, relationships are threatening because there is the risk of being totally engulfed by the other person. Since they lack ontological security, the schizoid often draws away from the world and retreats into their own mind. The problem, however, is that even their own minds are split. Since they don't have a stable sense of Self, they never experience that sense of integration or unity, either while they are alone or when they are with other people.

Laing makes anoteher interesting point. He says that it is not so strange that these patients feel the way they do. It may, in fact, be the normal people who are truly strange. Recall Freud's division of the human Self into three parts (id, ego, superego) or even McGilchrist's left and right brain split. What does it mean to have multiple subpersonalities, each with its own goals, competing in the same person? If a unity of a sense of Self does exist within the individual, to what extent is it real or authentic? What does it mean for one part of a person's

"Self" to address a different part of another person's "Self"?

The point here is that to function normally, there is a lot that "normal" people must inhibit or repress. There is a lot of inner conflict and Self-contradictions that need to be ignored. In the end, with all the chaos brought about by the "normal" – from the nuclear bomb to the pillage of nature, to genocides against fellow man, to the outright theft, manipulation, and aggression that goes on in corporations, bureaucracies, and institutions – the supposed epitome of sanity in society, one must wonder, like Laing, who is really insane?

Narcissism

From Statistics to Mass Indoctrination

There is a problem that occurs when we think of the world in terms of statistics. It leads us to treat individuals as "anonymous units that pile up in mass formations." As a result, moral responsibility shifts from the individual to the state. Instead of "moral and mental differentiation of the individual, you have public welfare and the raising of the living standard." The result is that people do not derive their goals and meaning from individual development, but through the state.

*"The individual is increasingly
deprived of the moral decision
as to how he should live his own
life, and instead is ruled, fed,
clothed and educated as a
social unit, accommodated in
the appropriate housing unit,
and amused in accordance with
the standards that give pleasure
and satisfaction to the masses."*

*The Undiscovered Self, Carl
Jung*

After the state is given responsibility for
everything, certain individuals take power of the
state. And the masses – an unorganized,
formless entity in desperate need for order,
willingly resigns its autonomy to the individuals
in power, the ruling elite. This gives rise to
dictatorships and authoritarian regimes. The
state becomes a pseudo personality, from whom
everything is expected. But it is merely a
camouflage for those few individuals who have
figured out how to manipulate it.

And as the crowd grows larger, the individual
becomes more negligible. Statistical truths and
large numbers marginalize the importance of the
individual personality – "that is not represented
and personified by any mass organization." Jung
recalls a thoughtful comment by his friend, "Here
you have the most convincing reason for not

believing in immortality: all those people want to be immortal!"

When confronted with large numbers, the individual falls into a state of awe, to such an extent that they undermine their own individual beliefs and desires. So, the individual feels insecure, and choose to "collectivize his responsibility" by handing his duties over to a corporation or a government body. The environment is so complex, that the individual feels compelled to relieve himself of agency.

And here, again, we touch on the dilemma of connectedness vs disconnectedness. On one hand, the individual feels disconnected because their own individual experience is totally marginalized (in favor of averages), and on the other hand, the individual feels attached because they have forfeited their responsibility to a much larger and more powerful entity.

Jung thought that there was one defense against collectivization, and the elimination of the individual, and it was faith in God. Without faith as an anchor, there can be no resistance to the "physical and moral blandishments of the world." In other words, the world is filled with devices that cater to the ego of the individual and compel him to absolve his own individuality. Intellectual or moral insight into the moral irresponsibility of the mass man is merely a negative recognition. It is a tearing down of an existing structure, but it does not replace it with anything else.

For this, Jung believed, the individual needed faith in God. The idea that man has become the master of his own destiny is an illusion. He is the "the slave and victim of the machines that have conquered space and time for him; he is intimidated and endangered by the might of the war technique which is supposed to safeguard his physical existence; his spiritual and moral freedom."

Human beings are not very good at understanding themselves psychologically. To do so – they must understand their subconscious selves. The mistake that churches have made is like that of the state – in trying to reduce the individual into nothing but a number – who's salvation lies in larger numbers. And the comfort given to man by organized religion will not provide him with the ability to change from within. To overcome mass delusion, man must become Self-reflective and courageous.

Men who ground their moral foundations in science are guilty of confusing scientific questions with metaphysical or moral ones, according to Jung.

"The imposing arguments of science represent the highest degree of intellectual certainty yet achieved by the mind of man. So at least it seems to the man of today, who has received hundred-fold enlightenment

*concerning the backwardness
and darkness of past ages and
their superstitions. That his
teachers have themselves gone
seriously astray by making false
comparisons between
incommensurable factors never
enters his head."*

*The Undiscovered Self, Carl
Jung*

Mass indoctrination is the total opposite of
individuality, since the individual is wholly
subjected to the well-being of the group. That is
why people like Jung fought against the
destruction of the individual. On the other hand,
there is the opposite problem, when the
individual thinks they are so important, that the
needs of the group are no longer relevant. That
is what we colloquially call "narcissism."

Dichotomy 17: The Fool and The Narcissist

The "fool" is an archetype in analytical
psychology – it is a very human disposition.
Whether a person can relate to himself with
tolerant humor depends on how foolish his
ideals and grandiose Self permit him to be.

Narcissists feel embarrassed and are always afraid of making a fool of themselves. This fear of not conforming well to what is expected of them, they feel completely humiliated when this happens. Most of these situations can be seen humorously, but because they are outside the 'conventional' framework', they shame some people.

To what extent do we have the courage to be spontaneous? This involves a risk, and this behavior may not be considered proper – it may seem out of place. But whether we feel we are being made a fool of or have a tolerant relationship to our foolish side to be able to laugh at ourselves depends on how well we identify with the fool archetype.

That is, whether the ego can distinguish itself from it while accepting its existence in our psyche. Humor may be a saving grace that allows us to tolerate our own weaknesses and help us maintain a healthy distance from our struggle for perfection.

Narcissists cannot behave this way since they rarely feel they are being taken seriously. They always hope for approval from others but suspect they are being rejected or ignored. They feel that as soon as they expose themselves, they will be made fun of.

This type of tension between fear and hope, between feelings of inferiority and feelings of grandiosity is part of the painful experience that has been elucidated in psychology by Adler under the term 'inferiority complex'.

The person that doesn't take things seriously or isn't taken seriously is very threatening to the narcissist. But sometimes, a counter reaction can happen where the narcissist takes the role of the class clown – as a sad way of defending themselves against ridicule. If they can be the source of the ridicule, if they can control it, then they cannot be made a fool by others.

Kohut saw wisdom as the capacity to accept the inevitable imperfection intellectually and emotionally in human nature.

Narcissists are often charming, they were taught at a young age to appease the narcissism of their parents, and this charm becomes used as a social tool to get other people to care for them. It may sometimes protect the individual from despair.

The Myth of Narcissus

Jung often said that people unconsciously 'live a myth'. It might equally be said that a myth lives within the people themselves, in their unconscious, motivating them to certain forms of experience and behavior.

Ovid wrote the story of Narcissus. He first introduces the seer Tiresias and then the nymph Liriope who gives birth to an exceptionally beautiful son who she named Narcissus. His father was the river god Cephisus, who forced the nymph into his stream and made her pregnant. When Tiresias was asked if Narcissus would have a long life he replied 'Yes, if he does not come to know himself.'

The nymph Echo falls passionately in love with Narcissus, who has become a hunter, but he does not love her. His pride was so unyielding that neither boys nor girls could touch him.

One day, he was seen by the talkative nymph who cannot be quiet when others speak. All she did was repeat the last words of the phrases she heard. She often wanted to flirt with him, but since she could never speak first, she failed at achieving her goal. Eventually, she disappears into the woods and never speaks again.

Narcissus then unwittingly falls in love with his own reflection.

Analysis of the Myth

Pausanias, the travel writer, did not think it was plausible that anyone would fall in love with himself in full awareness, so he postulated that Narcissus had a twin sister who he loved passionately.

When she died prematurely, he made a pilgrimage to the spring to see his own reflection in its waters. Although he knew that he was looking at an image of his own features, it provided him with some relief from his suffering, for he imagined that what he was seeing was the image of his sister.

This story is supposed to show us how absurd the older myth is, and without moralizing, introduces the incest motif. Even in the second century, there seemed to be a need to make the myth logically plausible.

Plotinus and the neo-Platonist interpretation of the myth is to see it as an allegory. According to this interpretation, the soul sinks into darkness when it dedicates itself to sensory beauty.

Narcissus stands for the soul in its pleromatic, pure form; submersion in water represents the soul's absorption into matter, the birth of the materialized form of existence that is at the same time an illusion – namely the materialized form of existence. Plotinus concentrated so much on spirituality that he was ashamed of having a body.

> *Francis Bacon in the early seventeenth century first made Narcissus a symbol of Self-love. He saw the phenomenon of Self-regard as being highly dubious, not without a positive side, since vanity and Self-love may inspire many accomplishments.*
>
> *Vinge*

Interpretation of the Myth from a Jungian Perspective

The hunting drive is antithetical to love or the god Eros. Strict parents often tell their children to not be diverted by romantic fantasies, so that they can be successful in their hunt for good grades at school.

When we aim at something that requires prolonged concentration, our partner's need for love becomes a disturbance. The partners of people who pursue difficult goals – in politics, industry, the arts could tell us a lot about how they had to relegate their own needs to encourage, assist, and pacify their striving partner. The people who feel inclined to hunt for special recognition in a field are rightly termed narcissistic. These people need partners as hunting companions who need to make as few of their own demands as possible, because these are Selfish, limiting, or smothering.

As Narcissus says, 'Away with these embraces! I would die before I would have you touch me!'

A final point Is that Narcissus sees a beautiful reflection of himself, and he has been loved for this beauty by his mother and others – with intensity. People with narcissistic problems tend to be admired from an early age for a physical or personality trait or special talent. This admiration is not for the child, but for his prized trait. The child feeds the narcissism of parents who see their children as an extension of themselves.

Jung said that if psychic contents remain unconscious, they will manifest themselves first in forms of projections. We often love others because they embody our best traits, and we hate the qualities in others that we cannot admit to having.

Jung and Kohut discovered that the failure of the individual to come to terms with his own finiteness is what leads to narcissistic problems

– such as the drive for prestige, possessiveness, and chronic dissatisfaction.

But being fascinated with one's own reflection can lead to Self-discovery. Through Self-knowledge, Self-realization, and becoming what you are, you can transcend the problems associated with narcissism.

Dichotomy 18: Inferiority vs Grandiosity

Kohut told us that all of us experience disappointment when we find out that our real-life parents are not perfect, omnipotent, or omniscient after all – and this can create a 'transmuting internalization.' The child deals with his break from the caring other by the idealization of the superego (parental values) – this maintains the child's Self-esteem and promotes his survival. People who devote themselves completely to worthwhile and meaningful tasks (scientific, artistic, religious, social) are examples of this.

In Kohut's view, there is an archaic 'grandiose Self' with archaic 'omnipotent' ideals and there is another Self which feels weak and inferior. For sound development, realistic ambitions and mature ideals are adopted. The resulting Self is bipolar: one pole operates with ambition, and demands admirations, while the other operates with meaningful goals and ideals. The 'tension gradient' between these poles is regulated through talent and skill. Ideally, the two poles work together.

There are few people who possess an intact ego-Self axis. A complex civilization makes too many demands on the ego and leads the individual to Self-alienation, which leads to the disruption of the ego-Self axis. Modern psychotherapy is the attempt to reconnect the ego to the Self, or to its inner nature.

Jung and Kohut got their insights from different places. Jung got his from archaic symbolism, personal experiences, images from the unconscious, and the psychology of religion. Kohut came to his conclusions through empathizing with his clients and introspection. He was not influenced by Jung.

Both Jung and Kohut saw that the ideal was to seek balance, rather than fall into either extreme of the dichotomies. The dichotomies were not identical, but both wrote of a schism between the practical and the meaningful, and the need to reconcile the two.

The Narcissistic Personality of our Time

In modern times, we think of Narcissus as the person who is too interested in how they look, are entitled, admire themselves too much, lack empathy, and have an excessive need for attention from others.

This leads to the irrefutable conclusion that each person is somewhat of a narcissist. Freud wrote a famous paper on the subject, "*On Narcissism: An Introduction*." According to Freud, the ego develops during infancy at the oral stage of the psychosexual development. At this point, the child thinks he is the center of the universe, and for good reason – his mother fulfils every need he has.

But as he gets older, he notices that not everything goes his way, so his Self-centeredness recedes. Freud noticed this and concluded that each person has some level of narcissism that is important for normal psychological development. After early childhood, our total Self-love begins to decrease, and our love for others takes its place.

There are two types of narcissism, and they relate to libidinal energy. The child's libidinal energy is directed inside the newly developed ego – this is called ego-libido. During this time, ego-instincts (need for Self-preservation) and sex-instincts (need to preserve the species) are inseparable. This Self-love is called Primary Narcissism and is what Freud considered necessary for a healthy psyche.

But with time, the ego becomes filled with libidinal energy, which it has been receiving since childhood, so it looks for outside objects to direct all this energy. That is when sex-instincts separate from ego-instincts. So now, the individual's energy is both directed towards his ego (autoerotism) and towards other objects (or object-libido).

Inevitably, object-love is not reciprocated, and this results in a trauma that prevents more libidinal energy from flowing outward. The individual regresses to a childlike state, where all libidinal energy flows back towards the ego.

Then the individual is consumed in neurotic Self-love. This was called Secondary Narcissism by Freud, and it may lead to Paraphrenia (combination of megalomania and paranoid delusions).

When people direct love to others, they diminish the amount of energy available for themselves. If this love is not returned, they will think of the world as unworthy of their love. So, they might become Self-absorbed, and delusional.

People react to the contents of their unconscious in two ways, the first Is to lose Self-confidence and to resign their fate fully to their unconscious. The second feel an unpleasant increase of Self-confidence and conceit.

A grandiose Self craves admiration – it requires followers to have faith in its convictions to believe in its value. The individual's craving of his own greatness serves as a protection against 'gnawing doubts.' But he becomes sensitive to the slightest disapprobation and is always assuming the role of the one who is misunderstood and mistreated. He and his environment will pay dearly for this.

In ancient Greece, actors used masks to hide their faces, this is where Jung found the term 'persona' – it is to describe behavior connected to a specific role or occupation. But there is a danger in too strongly identifying with a persona – Self-esteem would be nourished only by collective roles rather than be grounded in genuine individuality. Often, people who do not gain Self-esteem from their individuality tend to associate with celebrities or people that do.

The Triumph of the Therapeutic

'But why on earth', you may ask 'should it be necessary for man to achieve, by hook or by crook, a higher level of consciousness?' This is truly the crucial question, and I do not find the answer easy. Instead of a real answer I can only make a confession of faith; I believe that, after thousands and millions of years, someone had to realize that this wonderful world of mountains and oceans, suns and moons, galaxies and nebulae, plants and animals, exists.

Jung (1939)

Jung wrote that the world is a large, meaningless machine without the reflecting consciousness of man. His confession of faith makes him an easy target for scientific psychologists who accuse him of lacking a scientific method. Kohut exonerates himself from the same accusation by stating:

There are those, of course, who might say that the aforementioned issues are not a legitimate subject matter of science; that by dealing with them we are leaving the areas that can be illuminated through scientific research and are entering the foggy regions of metaphysics. I disagree. Such issues as experiencing life as meaningless despite external success, experiencing life as meaningful despite external failure, the sense of a triumphant death or of a barren survival, are legitimate targets of scientific psychological investigation because they are not nebulous abstract speculations but the content of intense experiences that can be observed, via empathy, inside and outside the clinical situation.

Kohut, 1977: 242

Now, let us depart from the psychoanalysts, and analyze on a cultural and social level, the effect of psychoanalysis – the demystification of man's instincts and the explaining away of his religious yearnings, on society. Let us recall what the world used to look like prior to the advent of psychotherapy, and where it has moved towards since.

We begin with *The Triumph of the Therapeutic* by Phillip Rieff.

Rieff describes modern society (the book was written in 1966) as completely different from the past. Previously, society was marked by "religious man" – and then, many centuries later, by "economic man", and now, in the current stage, by "psychological man."

And this new type of individual differs from ancestors in the way he creates meaning in his life. Whereas the older generations sought meaning from without, by burdening themselves with cultural traditions and economic aspirations, the psychological man is mainly interested in maintaining a balanced mindset, he seeks meaning from within. A principal feature of psychological man is his indifference.

> *No longer the Saint, but the instinctual Everyman, twisting his neck uncomfortably inside the starched collar of culture, is the communal ideal, to whom men offer tacit prayers for deliverance from their inherited renunciations. Freud sought only to soften the collar; others, using bits and pieces of his genius, would like to take it off.*

To sum up Freud's observation, we can think of society as made up of controls and releases. A cultural revolution, such as the one we are experiencing (a revolution unfolds over a large time span, of decades and not months or years), then the releases overwhelm the system of controls. The rise of Christianity was an example of such a revolution.

Near the end of the 19th century, Western culture became more remissive (a sign of an imminent cultural revolution). But unlike previous revolutions, the new culture does not have a new set of commitments.

> *Western culture is changing
> already into a symbol system
> unprecedented in its plasticity
> and absorptive capacity.
> Nothing much can oppose it
> really, and it welcomes all
> criticism, for, in a sense, it
> stands for nothing.*

> *The Triumph of the Therapeutic,
> Rieff*

This vacuum is filled by Freud and psychoanalysis. Let us recall that Freud thought that psychological problems resulted from a triangular conflict between the id, ego, and super-ego. The old culture solved this tension by influencing the super-ego and crushing the id. The new culture, since it requires nothing from the individual, relaxes pressure on the super-ego, and allows the individual to be free.

> *Culture is another name for a design of motives directing the Self outward, toward those communal purposes in which alone the Self can be realized and satisfied.*
>
> *The Triumph of the Therapeuti, Rieff*

But the cost of freedom was a loss of meaning. A Culture of commitments offers a consolation for the misery of living because binding social commitments, while painful on many, holds out the promise of salvation. Christian culture offered its adherents a religious answer. Marxist culture offered its adherents an economic answer (the workers' paradise). The psychological culture offers no mechanism for salvation since it is individualistic. This marks the impoverishment of Western culture, according to Rieff.

While the old culture cured man's psychological needs by giving him a communal purpose, the new culture encourages Self-absorption and minimal group commitment. Blinding loyalties are taboo. Psychological man stands for nothing, in congruence with Freud's psychology of analysis and detachment.

Analysis impels the individual to understand but not to judge. And since there is hierarchy between our competing instincts, we must give expression to all. The ultimate purpose is to prevent the negotiations from breaking down.

Freud thought that the person who questioned the meaning and value of life was sick, since objectively, neither exist. To the person who accepts Freud's account, analysis appears rational, saving the individual from the pointless bustle which animated the lives of his ancestors.

The old answers to the deepest questions of life are useless.

Thus, Freud created a major change in Western society.

His ideas were the anti-creed for those who think of themselves as post-religious. But Freud refused to tell them what to pursue. He was only interested in giving them the tools to structure their inner life, even if the newly discovered structure is more imprisoning than what came before.

Freud proposed sublimation as the antidote to a meaning crisis – that is, to seek redemption through art and work as outlined in the previous examples. Here, Rieff quotes Harry Sullivan, a sage among psychologists, who said, "If you tell people how they can sublimate, they can't sublimate." The dynamics of culture are in the unwitting parts of it.

Now our renunciations have failed us; less and less is given back bettered. For this reason, chiefly, I think, this culture, which once imagined itself inside a church, feels trapped in something like a zoo of separate cages. Modern men are like Rilke's panther, forever looking out from one cage into another. Because the modern sense of identity seems outraged by imprisonment in either old church or new cage, it is the obligation of sociologists, so far as they remain interested in assessing the quality of our corporate life, to analyze doctrinal as well as organizational profiles of the rage to be free of the inherited morality, the better to see how these differ from what is being raged against.

Rieff, The Triumph of the Therapeutic

But in the end, Rieff concedes that there is no way of knowing whether the anti-creed of Freud is a gift or a curse – we will have to wait and see.

Indeed, with the arts of psychiatric management enhanced and perfected, men will come to know one another in ways that could facilitate total socialization without a symbolic of communal purpose. Then the brief historic fling of the individual, celebrating himself as a being in himself, divine and therefore essentially unknowable, would be truly ended—ending no less certainly than the preceding personifications of various renunciatory disciplines. Men already feel freer to live their lives with a minimum of pretense to anything more grand than sweetening the time. Perhaps it is better so; in cultures past, men sacrificed themselves to heroic and cruel deceptions, and suffered for glories that once mirrored their miseries. Not until psychological men overcome lives of squalor can they truly test their assumption that the inherited ideals of glory are no longer required.

Rieff, The Triumph of the Therapeutic

Jung, Reich, and Lawrence – disciples of Freud – established their own pseudo-religious systems of thought – simulations of religion. Rather than become completely anti-religious, like their predecessor, they were determined to provide "something" in place of "nothing" – but according to Rieff, all three were intellectually inferior to Freud.

Jung, as we have explored, proposed a religious psychology, a deity through the amalgam of archetypes that exist in the collective unconscious; Reich introduced radical political activism as the means to Self-fulfillment; and Lawrence proposed erotic experience as a therapy to integrate the Self. Each rejects the past, but each seeks a new definition of man.

In the aftermath of the psychoanalytic movement, the anti-religions and the pseudo religions, Rieff wonders if the age-old question posed by Dostoevsky "Can civilized men believe?" ought to be replaced by its inverse "Can unbelieving man be civilized?"

> *We believe that we know something our predecessors did not: that we can live freely at last, enjoying all our senses— except the sense of the past— as unremembering, honest, and friendly barbarians all, in a technological Eden.*

The Culture of Narcissism

The Culture of Narcissism by Christopher Lasch
was published in 1979. Lasch argued that the
"me generation" that Tom Wolfe previously
celebrated, a new era when the individual finally
differentiated themselves from the demands of
the group, was in fact, dysfunctional, empty, and
worthy of contempt.

He bases his argument on Sigmund Freud's
insights, who wrote an important paper on the
subject called, *On Narcissism*. At first, Lasch
points out a social paradox. People are
expected to submit to the rules of society, but
modern society refuses to ground these rules
into a moral code. The individual's reaction is to
become Self-absorbed, and far from feeling
elated or grandiose, he loses Self-efficacy and
Self-worth. The Self shrinks back towards a
passive state in which the world remains
unformed.

*The egomaniacal, experience-
devouring imperial Self
regresses into a grandiose,
narcissistic, infantile, empty
Self: a "dark wet hole" as
Rudolph Wurlitzer writes in Nog,*

"where everything finds its way sooner or later. I remain near the entrance, handling goods as they are shoved in, listening and nodding.

The Culture of Narcissism, Lasch

He then borrows a term from Phillip Rieff, the author of *The Triumph of the Therapeutic,* the term "psychological man." Who is the psychological man? He is the modern individual, who has cut himself off from his roots, and from his past. He is plagued by anxiety, depression, vague discontents, and a sense of inner emptiness.

He seeks neither Self-aggrandizement nor spiritual transcendence but peace of mind, under conditions that increasingly work against it. Whereas man used to look towards priests, Self-help preachers, or models of success such as successful business leaders, his main ally in the struggle for composure is now the therapist. The modern equivalent to salvation is "mental health."

Therapy has established itself as the successor both to rugged individualism and to religion; but this does not mean that the "triumph of the therapeutic" has become a new religion in its

*own right. Therapy constitutes
an antireligion, not always to be
sure because it adhreres to
rational explanation or scientific
methods of healing, as its
practitioners would have us
believe, but because modern
society "has no future" and
therefore gives no thought to
anything beyond its immediate
needs.*

*The Culture of Narcissism,
Lasch*

The principal goal of the therapist is not help you carve out a future, but to sedate you. He does not want you to look forwards, but to focus on your emotions in the present. The idea here is not that the therapist should be responsible for fulfilling these functions – it is not his job to do this. But since therapy has taken over the role of religion in alleviating man's angst about the future and the purpose of his life, it is tasked with the heavy burden of giving people good answers, and in empowering them.

Yet, Lasch argues that it does the opposite, it reduces man further and further. Even meaning and love, to the therapist, are not valuable in themselves, but useful insofar as they fulfil the patient's emotional needs.

The post-Freudian therapies attempt to rid the individual from the ideas of love and duty, and for whom mental health means gratifying each impulse and removing all inhibitions.

Impending Disaster

Near the turn of the twentieth century, there was a growing conviction that everything was coming to an end. And people were so sure of a catastrophic event, a nuclear war, that people gave up on looking for a solution, and instead, kept themselves busy with survival strategies designed to prolong their lives, or programs that ensured good health and peace of mind.

After the political turmoil of the sixties, Americans have retreated to purely personal preoccupations. Having no hope of improving their lives in any of the ways that matter, people have convinced themselves that what matters is psychic Self-improvement: getting in touch with their feelings, eating health food, taking lessons in ballet or bellydancing, immersing themselves in the wisdom of the East, jogging, learning how to "relate," overcoming the "fear of pleasure." Harmless in themselves, these pursuits, elevated to a program and wrapped in the rhetoric of authenticity and awareness,

signify a retreat from politics and
a repudiation of the recent past.

The Culture of Narcissism,
Lasch

After displacing religion as the organizing framework of American culture, the therapeutic outlook threatens to displace politics. Lasch discusses the political revolutionaries of the sixties, such as Abbie Hoffman and his associate, Jerry Rubin, who decided (a decade later) that it was more important to get one's head together, and immerse themselves in therapeutic activities, than move multitudes.

Long lasting relationships have become more difficult. Relationships are framed in terms of combat. "assertiveness" "fighting fair" … Open relationships are more common. But they end up intensifying the disease they pretend to cure. The root of their problems is social. By refusing to commit or attach themselves to others, they presume that their problems have nothing to do with other people, and everything to do with their feelings.

There is the ego that is healthy, it contains the healthy judgements of others and superior ideals to strive towards. The sadistic superego is the archaic and destructive force that is harsh and punishing. The superego is filled with destructive forces from early violent fantasies, which result from the parents' failure to satisfy all the fantasies of the child.

In a society, where there is a healthy disdain for authority, the superego softens, and forms into a harsh but constructive conscience. Whereas in a society that hates authority, the child grows up still thinking of their parents as devouring monsters and fails to develop a healthy superego.

Returning to Kohut, useful creative work which confronts the individual with unsolved intellectual and aesthetic problems, offers hope for the narcissist to transcend their predicament since it requires the individual think about problems that are outside the Self.

Recall that Freud revised his initial theory on narcissism. He first concluded that the libido was comprised of Self-love. He changed his mind and concluded that the id was in fact, the great reservoir of the libido. He acknowledged the existence of non-sexual drives, such as aggression or the death instinct, and the alliance between the Ego and the Id, ego, and aggression. This is important, because the way in which you define narcissism determines how and to what extent you recognize narcissism in society.

The narcissist does not love himself but is defending himself against aggressive impulses.

Those who deny the psychological dimension also deny the character traits

*associated with pathological
narcissism, which in less
extreme form appear in such
profusion in the everyday life of
our age: dependence on the
vicarious warmth provided by
others combined with a fear of
dependence, a sense of inner
emptiness, boundless repressed
rage, and unsatisfied oral
cravings. They also do not
discuss what might be called the
secondary characteristics of
narcissism: pseudo Self-insight,
calculating seductiveness,
nervous, Self-deprecatory
humor.*

*The Culture of Narcissism,
Lasch*

Thus, they deprive themselves of any basis on which to make connections between the narcissistic personality type and certain characteristic patterns of contemporary culture, such as the intense fear of old age and death, altered sense of time, fascination with celebrity, fear of competition, decline of the play spirit, deteriorating relations between men and women. For these critics, narcissism remains at its loosest a synonym for Selfishness and at its most precise a metaphor, and nothing more, that describes the state of mind in which the world appears as a mirror of the Self.

In short, Lasch defines contemporary man as disconnected from traditional methods of connecting with the world. The triumph of the therapeutic sensibility, particularly in the US, has resulted in a Self-obsessed individual, who has no care for posterity, idealizes youth and perfection, requires constant adulation and praise, worships fame and celebrity, despises old age and weakness, hates dependence on others yet need their warmth, has pseudo Self-insight, sees the world as a reflection of themselves, doesn't want lasting relationships, doesn't want lengthy commitments, feels empty, is a hypochondriac due to aggression directed inwards, desires the illusion of success and competence, rather than success and competence.

The narcissist thinks that people are disposable, usable, not important, and have faux intelligence, that is, he is good at intellectualizing but only to evade, for example by rephrasing what the other person said, rather than trying to find truth. He tries to defend ego from libidinal (non-sexual) forces, including death drive and aggression, disdains all forms of authority, worships consumerist culture, think it is more important to be worshipped by others than to be content, makes no real effort to understand the world.

The Rise of the Nones

The belief of modern society, and perhaps even more so in the future, with the recent rise of techno-utopianism (man's ultimate salvation depends on a technical progress), is the belief that a combination of multiple autophile behaviors will be an adequate substitute for traditional communities and social contracts – that impel the individual to direct their libidinal energy away from the ego.

In the past, when people directed this energy outwards, it grounded them and gave them a sense of humility. In today's more Self-centered world, the individual believes that the community owes them something. That is not to say that the community does not owe the individual, a hard-working member, anything for their efforts. But it is the attitude that is in question.

In the modern world, it is not so much the cult leaders or religious leaders that are worshipped anymore, but the technologists in Silicon Valley that promise a post human utopia, or the meditation/wellness enterprises that sell you a selection of spiritual products for a monthly subscription with a money-back-guarantee. The modern narcissist worships many new forms of religion.

If you've ever been to a yoga studio or a CrossFit class, ever practiced "Self-care" with a ten-step Korean beauty routine or a Gwyneth Paltrow–sanctioned juice

cleanse, ever written or read
Internet fan fiction, ever compared
your spiritual outlook to a
Dungeons and Dragons
classification ("lawful good, chaotic
evil") or your personal
temperament to that of a
Hogwarts house, ever channeled
your sense of cosmic purpose into
social justice activism, ever tried to
"bio-hack" yourSelf or used a
meditation app like Headspace,
you've participated in some of
these trends...

*Strange Rites: New Religions
for a Godless World. Tara
Isabella Burton*

Burton describes the new kinds of cults that
have emerged in the modern world, particularly
in the U.S. She describes the phenomenon of
"remixed religions." Before internet forums
existed, an individual was handed down a
traditional set of beliefs that they would then
pass on to their children, and if they chose not
to, they would lead secular lives, often isolated.
Seldom would they find like-minded people.

In the internet age, the picture looks quite
different. Burton takes us back to 2001.

After 9/11, Jerry Falwell, the provocateur of the religious right, blamed the attacks on "the pagans, and the abortionists, and the feminists, and the gays and lesbians" and the liberals who tried to "secularize America." Sam Harris, the atheist intellectual, predicted 5 years later (in an interview with Wired magazine) that the America he lived in was a secular nation, as opposed to America decades or centuries ago. The Four Horsemen of the New Atheist movement, which includes Harris, Hitchens, Dawkins, Dennet lauded the modern rise of secularism. In other words, both sides agreed. Compared to the America that existed half a century ago, or 300 years ago, modern America had become a secular nation. Some saw it as a sign of Armageddon, others saw is as a triumph of science and reason.

But what do the numbers say? Is America more secular? Burton presents the numbers. In 2007, 15 percent of Americans called themselves religiously unaffiliated (not part of any traditional organized religion). By 2012, the number went up to 20 percent (and to 30 percent for adults under 30). Now, those numbers are even higher. Around 25 percent of Americans say they have no religion, and when looking at millennials (those born after 1990) – those numbers reach almost 40 percent.

The religious Nones, as they are known, are the biggest religious demographic in America, and the fastest growing one. As a group, they outnumber white evangelicals (who only make up 15 percent of the population).

At first, one gets the impression that Falwell and Harris were both right, America had truly become a secular nation. But Burton looks a little closer. While more Americans say they don't belong to an organized religion, that doesn't mean they aren't spiritual, or even that they don't believe in a Judeo-Christian God. Only around 7 percent of Americans identify as "atheist" or "agnostic." Most say they're "nothing in particular." 72 percent of Nones say they believe in either the God of the Bible or something else.

According to a 2018 Pew Research Center study, fifty five percent of the religiously unaffiliated believe in a higher power or spiritual force distinct from that described in the Judeo-Christian Bible. Furthermore, an additional seventeen percent of the unaffiliated said that they believed precisely in the God of the Abrahamic Bible. Forty-six percent of those Nones talk to God, or this higher power, regularly, and thirteen percent say that God talks back. Forty-eight percent of them think that a higher power has protected them throughout life. Forty-one percent say that it has rewarded them. Twenty-eight percent say it has punished them. Forty percent experience a sense of "spiritual peace and well-being" at least once a week—a percentage that actually increased by five points between 2007 and 2014. Forty-seven percent believe in the presence of "spiritual energy" in physical objects. Forty percent believe in psychics. Thirty-eight percent in reincarnation. Thirty-two percent in astrology. And sixty two percent, it turns out, in at least one of those four.

Strange Rites, Tara Isabella Burton

There are two ways of interpreting this data. On the one hand, you can see the rise of the Nones as a symbol of the breakdown of traditional Judeo-Christian religions. While many Nones are not totally secular, they are still nowhere near as religious as previous generations. And with time, the trend will continue in that direction. But the numbers reveal something else – few people are willing to make the leap to atheism. Even though it has never been more convenient to be an atheist, most Nones still maintain a belief, however loosely structured, in the supernatural.

The larger phenomenon that Burton studies throughout the rest of the book, is not so much a focus on the Nones, but on the phenomenon of 'remixed religions.' Even those who do belong to traditional religions have dabbled in 'remixing.'

3

THE DICHOTOMY OF THE FINITE AND THE INFINITE

Chapter 5: The Crowd

So far, we have discussed the various schools of psychoanalysis and psychology, how they started and what they teach us. We we have studied the various dichotomies that the individual experiences. We have learned about the rise of the Nones, the social developments that have taken place with the advent of psychoanalysis and the decline of traditional religion, including the rise of narcissism, polarization, and transhumanism. We must not forget the rise of nationalism in the 20th century. We have taken a brief tour through the history of mental illness, and we have learned about the various shortcomings of the psychological sciences.

In this part, we will look at an overlooked aspect of human nature, that may do more to explain the root of our desires, the origin of conflict, and the direction of technology and politics than any other psychological theory. It has been called "interpersonal psychology" by some. At the root of this intellectual development is a French literary critic named Rene Girard. But before we delve into Girard's "Mimetic Theory", and see how it relates to the modern world, we will survey some of the ideas that came before Girard.

We will start with Gustave Le Bon, the author of *The Crowd: A Study of the Popular Mind*.

The Popular Mind

Gustave Le Bon makes the point that when individuals join a crowd, they form a single being, or a mental unity. And no matter who the individuals are, once they are in a crowd, they become possessed by a collective mind that makes them think and behave in a way that is different than the way they would think and behave if they were alone.

What are the features of a crowd? They can only understand simple and extreme ideas. To the crowd, opinions are either absolute truths or absolute errors - as is always the case with beliefs induced by a process of suggestion rather than reasoning. Crowds are more likely to commit criminal acts. The savage and destructive instincts that are dormant in the individual but dangerous for him to commit by himself suddenly become permissible when he is part of a group. The group gives him the liberty to act freely on his instincts. Freud observed that aggressive feelings were kept in check by society, but in the same way that the collective can inhibit the individual, it can free the individual.

Another feature of the crowd is that they do not properly absorb the facts of reality. They see only apparent connections between things, they are immune to reason.

The epidemic of influenza,
which caused the death but a
few years ago of five thousand

persons in Paris alone, made
very little impression on the
popular imagination.

The Crowd: A Study of the
Popular Mind, Gustave Le Bon

Since there was no visible image, but merely bland weekly statistics, the emotions of the crowd are not stirred. A virus that kills thousands of people has less emotional impact than a dramatic spectacle, such as the fall of the Eiffel Tower, even if the latter has less than a hundred casualties. This philosophical speculation is corroborated by modern psychological research. In *Thinking: Fast and Slow*, Kahneman calls this phenomenon "availability bias."

There is one more feature of the crowd that Le Bon mentions, and it is that crowds are never interested in the truth.

The masses have never thirsted
after truth. They turn aside from
evidence that is not to their
taste, preferring to deify error, if
error seduce them. Whoever
can supply them with illusions is
easily their master; whoever

attempts to destroy their
illusions is always their victim.

The Crowd: A Study of the
Popular Mind – Gustave Le Bon

In another book *The Psychology of Revolution*, Le Bon argues that a revolution is the work of believers. It is hated by some and praised by others and is a dogma that is either accepted or rejected as a whole, without the use of logic.

Reason may spark a revolution, but it can only develop by mystic and emotional elements. A revolution often begins because of the suppression of crying abuses or a despotic government, or an unpopular state. The rational individual can point to the abuses of the government, but to move masses of people, its hopes must be awakened. Reason alone cannot accomplish this.

Sudden political revolutions are often the least important. They fizzle out quickly. Changing the name of a government does not change the mentality of a people. The true revolutions that transform the destinies of people are often done so slowly that historians can hardly point to their beginnings. It is more like evolution than revolution.

Le Bon divides revolutions according to three types: religious, scientific, and political.

The man who is hypnotized by his faith becomes an apostle ready to sacrifice his interests, happiness, and life for the triumph of his faith. The absurdity of his belief does not matter. To him, it is a burning reality. Political revolutions can only result from beliefs established in the minds people but can be caused by other things.

Discontent, when it is generalized, forms a party that is strong enough to struggle against the government. In countries with corrupt or incompetent rulers, hatred and disillusionment are sufficient to unite a people towards one mission.

But contrary to what you may think, the most conservative people are addicted to the most violent revolutions. They are not comfortable with gradual change. Their conservatism makes it difficult for them to evolve slowly or adapt to variations in the environment.

People never direct a revolution or conceive of them; they are compelled to act by their leaders. Only when their direct interests are affected do we see a fraction of people rise spontaneously. A movement this localized is a mere riot.

Revolution is easy when leaders are highly influential. But new ideas penetrate people very slowly. Generally, people accept a revolution without knowing why, and by the time they do understand why, the revolution would have faded away.

The great strength of revolutionary principles was that they gave a free reign to primitive, barbaric instincts which were restricted by secular and inhibitory action of law, tradition, and environment. As Freud taught, aggression and sexuality are the primary instincts repressed by man. In times of social chaos, the individual is given a rare opportunity to manifest these basic instincts.

The motto of Liberty, Equality, Fraternity, a true manifestation of hope and faith at the beginning of the Revolution, soon merely served to cover a legal justification of the sentiments of jealousy, cupidity, and hatred of superiors, the true motives of crowds unrestrained by discipline. This is why the Revolution so soon ended in disorder, violence, and anarchy.

The Psychology of Revolution, Gustave Le Bon

Therefore, the liberation of popular passion is dangerous. Once the torrent escapes from its bed, it does not return until it achieves widespread devastation.

"Woe to him who stirs up the dregs of a nation," said Rivarol at the beginning of the Revolution. "There is no age of enlightenment for the populace."

Le Bon noticed the conflict between the individual and the leader. Freud focused on the conflict between man's instincts and the norms of society. As a psychoanalyst, he observed how people already dealt with this issue through sublimation. Jung focused on the conflict between man's ethical and moral responsibilities, and the actions of a state. He also explained man's basic predicament, of being disconnected from the archetypes of the collective unconscious, and from his deep religious instinct. Jung's proposed solution was Individuation, which is a process that takes place slowly over the course of a person's life.

Freud acknowledged many of Le Bon's insightful points, but ultimately, he felt that Le Bon's theory failed to explain the secret behind the power of the leader. Le Bon focuses on the psychology of the crowd, and its various features, but he missed a crucial ingredient, the total devotion to the leader or figurehead. Freud explains this through his theory of the libido.

The libido binds the individual to the leader and convinces him to give up his individuality.

Different types of crowds exist. There are unorganized, transient crowds, but also artificial and durable crowds, such as the church and the army, and in these cases, there is an illusion that the leader loves the individuals. But these libidinal manifestations cover the aggressive drives. When a group collapses, this aggressiveness is expressed in outbursts of violence. What truly binds people together are the basic feelings of envy and aggression, according to Freud.

Rene Girard would explain it in a different way altogether. In fact, he believed that Freud misinterpreted his observations. Girard argued that Freud's observations about human behavior were accurate and brilliant, but the latter was incapable of coming up with the right explanation.

Briefly, the reason why group infighting occurs after the group's collapse, is because of a scapegoating mechanism. This will be the subject of the next chapter, where we will see how Girard's mimetic theory has much to say about the dichotomy of the Self, the dilemma between connectedness and disconnectedness.

Imitation

Psychology, as a separate branch of science, was born in the end of the 19th century. At the time, Enlightenment thinking was the vogue, yet there was acknowledgement of the important role of imitation. Gabriel Tarde was the most notable imitation theorist of this early period, he published *The Laws of Imitation*, where he defines imitation as "every impression every impression of an inter-psychical photography, so to speak, willed or not willed, passive or active. If we observe that wherever there is a social relation between two living beings, there we have imitation in this sense of the word."

Tarde thought of imitation as a fact about people. Even complex behaviors and ideas were the offspring of imitation. This idea challenged the notion of an autonomous Self.

"We err in flattering ourselves that we have become less credulous and docile, less imitative, in short, than our ancestors. This is a fallacy, and we shall have to rid ourselves of it."

Gabriel Tarde

Tarde even compared human sociality to a state of hypnosis. Because of his work, and the work of many others, the subject of imitation became hot topic before the turn of the century, especially when discussing hypnosis and crowd behavior.

In the same year, William James, the American psychologist, published Principles of Psychology. Here, James classifies imitation as instinctual behavior operating early in infancy and essential to human nature. He said:

And from this time onward man is essentially the imitative animal. His whole civilization depends on this trait, which his strong tendencies to rivalry, jealousy, and acquisitiveness reinforce. 'Nil humani a me alienum puto,' is the motto of each individual of the species; and makes him, whenever another individual shows a power or superiority of any kind, restless until he can exhibit it himself. But apart from this kind of imitation, of which the psychological roots are complex, there is the more direct propensity to speak and walk and behave like others, usually without any conscious intention of so doing. And there is the imitative tendency which shows itself in large masses of men, and produces panics, and orgies, and frenzies of violence, and which only the rarest individuals can actively withstand. The nature and importance that James ascribes to imitation is remarkable.

But imitation was ignored by Freud as he developed his theory of psychoanalysis. And no one can deny his profound influence on the social sciences and popular culture. Like psychoanalysis, Skinner's behaviorism and Piaget's cognitive theories of development assumed that imitation was not an innate ability and did not play an important role in the elaboration of complex cognitive functioning. But since then, the discovery of mirror neurons in the field of neuroscience, and the many experiments in developmental psychology which are referenced in *Mimesis and Science*, confirm the primacy of imitation in cognitive development.

Before we move on discuss Girard's mimetic theory, let us go back to Gabriel Tarde, the French sociologist, and further elaborate on what he said. Tarde suggested that imitation was an inter-psychological process existed, and it can be conscious or unconscious and applies to individuals and groups.

The father is the lord and model for his son, and his son's imitation is a primal phenomenon. This imitation does not depend on cunning or force, but on prestige, a process Tarde compared with hypnotism.

He then explained that prestige does not come from intelligence or strength of will that has an invisible connection to sexuality. He stressed the role of the unconscious in mass psychology and described how they are united by either love or hatred. These teachings were popularized by Le Bon's *The Crowd.*

Recall that Le Bon's main point was that a person in a crowd loses their individuality and gains a part of the crowd's soul - the latter is intellectually inferior and is intrinsically malicious, although capable of heroism as well. When the crowd is united by either love or hatred, it is because it only understands absolute emotions and ideas.

Freud's ideas have remarkable similarity to these concepts, although there are key differences too. What Tarde called imitation was what Freud later called identification, as

Ellenberger points out in *The Discovery of the Unconscious.*

According to Tarde, these laws of imitation are universal laws that apply not only to the social sciences but also to the natural sciences (the living world and physical phenomena).

The general argument Tarde advances can be summarized as follows. In sharp contrast to Durkheim's approach, Tarde argues that social development is determined not by general laws of a vague, impersonal or transcendent nature, external to individuals, but rather by 'individual renovative initiatives', which could be described as inventions, discoveries or innovations. These innovations are spread by imitation. Thus the basic principles of social development are contained within the invention-imitation pairing. 'Socially, everything is just inventions and imitations'[ii]

But imitations are not just sources of innovation, but sources of conflict. When a person imitates another person, the latter becomes a rival, when they are competing for a scarce resource. Thus, the individual's relationship to others, or the group, is both that of bonding and alienation, innovation and destruction, life and death.

But a group has power and energy that is far greater than the individual, while the individual can think for themselves, or do they? If there is no age of enlightenment for the populace, can there be one for the individual?

The line of reasoning advanced by Le Bon is that individuals, unlike groups, can think for themselves. But what if individuals are merely imitating other individuals?

The Adventures of Tom Sawyer

One of the most famous examples of gullibility in fiction is Mark Twain's fence-paining scene in the novel The Adventures of Tom Sawyer. In that scene, Tom's guardian, Aunt Polly, orders him to whitewash a stretch of wooden fence (30 feet long, 9 feet high).

Tom sees Jim the slave and offers to switch chores with him. In exchange for Jim painting the fence, Tom would go fetch water from the community pump. But Jim says no. Aunt Polly had told him not to accept Tom's offer. She anticipated that Tom would probably try to avoid doing his chores.

Tom tries several more ploys, and finally, Jim starts to waver when Tom shows him his sore toe. Aunt Polly comes out and breaks up this conversation by beating Tom with her shoe. Tom later gets inspired when he sees Ben Rogers walking by. Tom begins to paint, very thoughtfully, acting as if he is totally absorbed by his painting. Ben comment about how it's unfortunate that Tom has to work instead of play and Tom replies, "What do you call work?" When Ben asks "Why ain't that work?" Tom replies "Well, maybe it is, and maybe it ain't. All I know, is it suits Tom Sawyer."

Ben asks "Oh come, now, you don't mean to let on that you like it?" to which Tom replies "Like it? Well I don't see why I oughtn't to like it. Does a boy get a chance to whitewash a fence every day?" Ben then begs Tom to let him paint, but Tom resists, finally relenting only when Ben offers him the rest of his apple.

When Ben got too tired, Tom lets Billy Fisher take over in exchange for a kite, Johnny Miller in exchange for a dead rat, and so on. Then, in the middle of the afternoon, from being a boy in poverty, with chores he had to do but did not want to, Tom was literally rolling in wealth. If he hadn't ran out of whitewash, he would have bankrupted every boy in the village.

Tom reflects on the afternoon's experience and derives a general law of human behavior, "namely, that in order to make a man or a boy covet a thing, it is only necessary to make the thing difficult to attain."

People engage in various unpleasant and difficult recreational activities mainly because the "privilege costs them considerable money."

Chapter 6: Mimetic Theory

Imitation is copying the other person. Mimesis is copying what the other person wants. Mimetic conflict happens in a way that could be unrecognizable as imitation, but accurately recognizable as mimesis. If a subject and model are rivals, they don't copy what the other does, but they try to attain the end goal of one another. So, if the model's goal is to get rich quick, or gain social influence, or being feared. Then the subject would not replicate the exact behaviors but find ways of obtaining the objects.

So, the model may be trying to get rich quick by investing in speculative stocks. The subject may visit the casino more frequently than they like. If the model tries to participate in their local political organizations to gain social influence, the subject may spend time with disenfranchised groups of people and provide humanitarian assistance. If the model tries to instill fear in others by maintaining a domineering attitude, it a threatening tone, the subject may suddenly become interested in buying guns, or acting irreverently to authority.

The more different they try to be, the more similar they become. And the more similar they become, the more different they seem.

Dichotomy 17: The Dichotomy of Autonomy and Mimesis

Where do man's desires come from? The psychoanalysts have proposed that aggression, sexuality, religious instincts, the need for creative expression are universal instincts. Recall the discussion in the first part of the book by referring to Erich Fromm, where I discussed not just how these instincts were essential for life, but often took precedence over the urge to live (hence why many have committed suicide, that is, they chose to override their instinct to survive because of their failure to satisfy and non-instinctual passion (love, fame, revenge).

But why do we want the things we do? What makes one individual attached to this sports team, this piece of artwork, or that film or music album? Aside from making a living, what moves a person to dedicate their lives to a career path, to the attainment of professional awards and glories, to the achievement of fame and recognition, often at the expense of health, sanity, and peace of mind? In other words, where do these non-instinctual desires come from? And why are they so powerful?

One thinker who discovered a simple yet powerful answer to this question was Rene Girard, a literary theorist who spent decades looking for a unifying theory in literature (to understand what truly motivated people). He does not claim to have originated *Mimetic Theory*, but that he discovered it in the greatest works of literature.

Instead of focusing on what makes literary works stand apart, which is what literary theorists usually do, Girard wanted to find what they all have in common, because it is only the great writers that succeed in representing the mechanisms of human behavior faithfully, without distortion. The greater the writer, the less variable are the human systems of relationships, and the more truthful they are.

It is the feeling for the general in the potential writer, which selects material suitable to a work of art because of its generality. He only pays attention to others, however dull and tiresome, because in repeating what their kind say like parrots, they are for that very reason prophetic birds, spokesmen of a psychological law."

Proust, A Remembrance of Things Past

Mimetic Theory not only seeks to explain why human beings are motivated to do things other than survive, but why conflict arises in the first place, why scapegoating is a universal phenomenon and why there is a tendency for people who are closer together to fight more frequently.

Girard says that we borrow our desires from other people. We are not autonomous beings that select for ourselves our own authentic goals. Our desire for an object (prestige, popularity) is provoked by the desire of a model (someone we aspire to be like) for this object. The subject does not directly desire the object, he desires the desire of the model.

There is an indirect triangular relationship between the subject, object, and the model.

Through the object, one is drawn to the model, whom Girard calls the mediator: it is in fact the model who is sought. Girard calls desire "metaphysical" in the measure that, as soon as a desire is something more than a simple need or appetite, "all desire is a desire to be", it is an aspiration, the dream of a fullness attributed to the mediator.

Mimesis can either be positive or negative. You can either emulate model's positive desires or negative desires.

If the model is a successful politician, you will emulate his desires, which is the recognition of his peers, fame, or vanity. These are negative traits. Positive traits to be emulated can be diligence, Self-sacrifice, and honor.

It is up to the subject to decide which traits are worth emulating. We speculate, and for good reason, that the less conscious the emulation, the less deliberate the process of carefully choosing to desire superior traits.

Competing Theories for Innate Desire

In one lecture, Girard explains his theory by contrasting it with the theories of three major thinkers in the 20th century; they include Freud, Marx, and Nietzsche. Freud said that man is driven by sexual desires (Eros) and the death instinct (Thanatos), and that he represses them. This is necessary for the functioning of civilization. Man must overcome this tendency by learning how to keep his instincts under control – to avoid the conflicts that result from this desire, or by channeling them towards socially useful pursuits (sublimation). The damaging effect of repression is neurosis.

Marx said that man's essential desire is economic, and the way to avoid conflict from the scarcity of wealth is to distribute it equally across the population. Nietzsche wrote that it is in fact power that drives man. And the solution is not to rationalize away his need for power, but to embrace it – to strive to become a 'superman' (ubermensch).

Girard can sympathize (although he does not agree) with Freud and Marx, since after they have diagnosed man's primary psychological drive, they opt for a solution, a way out of the dilemma so that peace is maintained. But Girard cannot sympathize with Nietzsche since the latter does not call for us to keep our desire for power in check, but to pursue it fully, at all costs.

In *The End of History and The Last Man*, Fukuyama explains the Hegelian idea of "the first man."

To some extent, Girard and Hegel agree that the source of human desires is the other. That is, the human being, a hyper-social creature, when he chooses to go beyond naturalistic desires such as food and shelter, must look to his fellow man as a source for his own desires.

For Girard, the other person is the source of desire because the subject desires what the other (model) desires. But for Hegel, this is a secondary consequence of something much more important. Man is really driven by recognition. And unlike Marx, who says that human motivation is a question of difference between the social classes, Hegel conceives of a man, like the man in "a state of nature" of Hobbes and Rousseau. Hegel's first man engaged in warfare with his fellow man.

This initial state of nature of all-against-all is a point that Girard, Hobbes, Rousseau, and Hegel agree about. But for Hegel and Girard, the idea of a social contract is rejected. And for Hegel, the first man was motivated by the need to be recognized by his adversary, and this can only be done by risking his own life (this proves that that the first man could overcome the biological prerogative to survive at all costs).

Pseudo-Narcissism

Sigmund Freud though that narcissism was a deviation of sexual libido, a damming up of libido within the ego so that it cannot flow outward toward objects. Freud thought narcissism was most often found in children and in women— what he called the eternal feminine type and he believed it added greatly to their appeal. But he did not explain this power of attraction. Girard critiques Freud by saying, "At no point does Freud admit that he might be dealing not with an essence but with a strategy, by which he himself has been taken in."

Girard thought that within narcissism exists a strategy, which is coquetry. The coquette understands desire better than Freud. She knows that desire attracts desire. To be desired, one must convince others than they desire themselves. If a woman who is narcissistic inspires desire in another person, that is because she pretends to desire herself – Freud interprets this as a form of circular desire where her libidinal energy is trapped. But her desire for herself makes her very tempting to the mimetic desire of others. If she desires herself, then others will want to desire her.

Freud mistakenly thought that the coquette is Self-sufficient, but Girard says that this is nonsense. She needs masculine desire to be directed at her, so that she can play her role as coquette. She feeds her own flame through the desire of others.

Thus, coquetry should be considered a kind of pseudo-narcissism.

In archaic societies, there were prohibitions that ensured a fair distribution of disposable objects among members of the culture. Girard gets the sense, that if they could, some of these cultures would have gotten rid of individual choice altogether, and therefore, completely get rid of mimetic rivalry.

But in modern society, the opposite takes place. There are no taboos that stop people from taking what is reserved for someone else. No initiation rites prepare individuals for necessary trials of life. Modern education does not warn the child that imitative behavior is sometimes encouraged, but at other times discouraged. Modern education does not reveal that there is no way of divining the future by simply observing the models themselves or to the objects that are desired.

Instead, it thinks it can resolve all problems by glorifying the natural spontaneity of desire, which is a purely mythological idea.

From Object Rivalry to Metaphysical Desire

In the same sense, Girard criticizes Freud for his Oedipal Complex. Below is an excerpt from *Things Hidden Since The Foundation of the World.* It is a conversation between Rene Girard and Guy Lefort.

R. G.: To untie the knot of desire, we have only to concede that everything begins in rivalry for the object. The object acquires the status of a disputed object and thus the envy that it arouses in all quarters, becomes more and more heated.

G. L.: Marxists will solemnly say that capitalism invented this escalation. Marxists hold that the problems we are discussing have been resolved once and for all by Marx, just as Freudians think that they have been resolved once and for all by Freud.

R. G.: As far as that goes, the real founders of capitalism, and also of the Oedipus complex, are the monkeys. All that capitalism, or rather the liberal society that allows capitalism to flourish, does, is to give mimetic phenomena a freer rein and to direct them into economic and technological channels. For religious reasons that are far from simple, capitalism is capable of doing away with the restraints that archaic societies placed upon mimetic rivalry. The value of an object grows in proportion to the resistance met with in acquiring it. And the value of the model grows as the object's value grows.

Even if the model has no particular prestige at the outset, even if all that 'prestige' implies-praestigia, spells and phantasmagoria-is quite unknown to the subject, the very rivalry will be quite enough to bring prestige into being. The mechanical character of primary imitation makes it likely that the subject will misinterpret the automatic aspect of his rivalry with the model. When the subject interrogates himself about this relationship of opposition, he will tend to endow it with meanings it does not possess. Moreover, all explanations that claim to be scientific, including those given by Freud, do the same.

Freud imagines that the triangle of rivalry conceals a secret of some kind, an 'oedipal' secret, whereas in fact it only conceals the rivalry's mimetic character. The object of desire is indeed forbidden. But it is not the 'law' that forbids it, as Freud believes-it is the person who designates the object to us as desirable by desiring it himself. The non-legal prohibition brought about through rivalry has the greatest capacity to wound and traumatize. This structure of rivalry is not a static configuration of elements.

Instead, the elements of the system react upon one another; the prestige of the model, the resistance he puts up, the value of the object, and the strength of the desire it arouses all reinforce each other, setting up a process of positive feedback. Only in this context does it become possible to understand what Freud calls 'ambivalence'-a pernicious force that he identified but was unable to explain adequately. Legal prohibitions are addressed to everyone or to whole categories of people, and they do not, as a general rule, suggest to us that we are 'inferior' as individuals. By contrast, the prohibition created by mimetic rivalry is invariably addressed to a particular individual, who tends to interpret it as hostile to himself." P. 295

Competition

Girard saw all forms of competition as stemming from a triangular system consisting of subject, model, and object. Freud introduced a theory of the Oedipal Complex, and thought that a scientific reading would lead us to believe that sons have a patricidal instinct. But Girard thinks that Freud, while correctly observing a pattern of behavior that prevails in many families, fails to recognize the true mechanism behind it. Like the coquette who narcissistically invites the other to desire what she desires. The Oedipal situation is no different. And neither is Capitalism which invites the individual to desire objects that others desire, and the more resistance there is, the stronger the desire.

Hobbes

Long before Girard, Hobbes had a different explanation of violence in *The Leviathan* by using fewer than a hundred words.

> So that in the nature of man, we find three principal causes of quarrel. First, competition; secondly, diffidence; thirdly, glory. The first maketh men invade for gain; the second, for safety; and the third, for reputation. The first use violence, to make themselves masters of other men's persons, wives, children, and cattle; the second, to defend them; the third, for trifles, as a word, a smile, a different opinion, and any other sign of undervalue, either direct in their persons or by reflection in their kindred, their friends, their nation, their profession, or their name.
>
> The Leviathan, Thomas Hobbes

Hobbes thought that competition was an unavoidable consequence of agents pursuing their interests. He also thought that we lacked freedom. Given that we lack freedom, and since we must compete if we are to further our interests, perpetual conflict is inevitable. Hence, "the condition of man… is a condition of war of everyone against everyone."

The problem with the Hobbesian and evolutionary account, is that it leaves no room for human agency. Indeed, Kant anticipated that the natural sciences would pose a great threat to human freedom, and he tackles this question in depth in *The Critique of Pure Reason.*

Hegel's First Man

But now let us move on from this point and go back to Hegel's first man. We should only assume that Hegel's definition of freedom is as described: man's ability to act against his own instincts. If he is right, then the Hobbesian and evolutionary narrative face a problem.

According to Hegel, there are three scenarios that can unfold in a state of nature, when man is in a war against man, and they are as follows: (1) They can both die, (2) one of them can die, or (3) one of them surrenders.

If they both die, then there is nothing to talk about. If one of them dies, then the survivor will be disappointed because he has gotten rid of the conscious being that would have recognized him as man. If the third scenario unfolds, and one of the men surrender, then the man who was willing to risk his life, who proved his freedom as a human being, becomes master. And the man that surrendered becomes slave.

Thus, a relationship develops between the two based on bondage and slavery. And here, the "free" man who proved that he could go against his instinct of Self-preservation is exalted.

This recognition by the other's superiority, of being truly human, truly free, is what drives human beings. The desire for recognition has two components. The first is basically Mimetic Theory: I desire what the other desires.

The second component is about the recognition of one's own humanity. "Because I defy death and fear and hunger (biological imperatives), you are forced to recognize me." In other words, I desire to be desired.

We now arrive to the conclusion of Hegel's thought about "the first man." Like Hobbes, he sees in human nature itself the cause of violence.

Man is a social animal, directed by others, but his sociability does not lead him into a peaceful civil society, but into a violent struggle to the death for pure prestige. For Girard, prestige is just a by-product of mimesis. What is missing in Girard is an explanation for why prestige is a meme that is desired in the first place. But Girard would simply say that the memes themselves are irrelevant, all that matters is the mimetic mechanism.

Hegel's account adds an additional layer. Not only are people mimetic, they are innately prestige-seeking. The reason why prestige is important is that human beings were born with the desire to be recognized by the other. But why were humans born with this instinct?

For Girard, it is easy to avoid this problem, since human beings are only born with the instinct to imitate (an animal instinct, but one that is taken to an extreme with human beings).

The Origin of Culture

A great overview of Girard's ideas *is Rene Girard's Mimetic Theory*, by Wolfgang Palaver. In a systematic, careful synthesis of Girard's thought, Palaver summarizes the mimetic insights that were derived from authors such as Dostoevsky, Shakespeare, Cervantes, Flaubert, and Proust. And finally, he shows the precise stories of the Old and New Testament that confirm Girard's thesis. What is Girard's thesis?

Man is fundamentally mimetic; he does not know what to desire, so he imitates the desires of others (models). If the models are internal (within his social sphere), he may reach a point of conflict with his model because they are both competing for the same desire (object). If the model is external (outside his social sphere), then there will be no conflict since there will be no rivalry. Because man is more mimetic than any other animal, he has the capacity to imitate abstractly. But the ability for abstract imitation was only earned after the discovery of the first instance of language, the first symbol.

A sketch of how this process occurred is outlined well in the book *The Palgrave Handbook of Mimetic Theory and Religion.* Here is a simplified version, which may also explain how the "initial" desire came about, lest we fear that the mimetic hypothesis leads us to postulate an infinite regress (or turtles all the way down).

First, whatever truth we can acknowledge about mimetic theory is observable in plain sight. If we want proof that our desires are mimetic, we have an entire world around us, and we can test the hypotheses laid forth. We would expect certain patterns of behavior to converge with what the theory would anticipate (internal mimesis, stronger rivalry than external mimesis, developmental psychology, mirror neurons, etc....)

As for an explanation, for how initial desires came about, let us review Girard's theory for the hominization of our species.

Some theorists have proposed that the reason we have advanced cognitive apparatus compares to chimpanzees and bonobos, for example, is that homo sapiens were Machiavellian. But as Girard noted, this begs the question. Why were homo sapiens Machiavellian in the first place?

Like Freud, Girard agreed that the beginning of culture occurred because of a primordial murder. Freud thought that this murder was patricidal (hence the Oedipal Complex), but Girard did not think that was true, as explained before.

Instead, Girard tells us that in the beginning, before society and language developed, when man found himself competing for resources with other men, in a state of all-against-all, a chance development occurred.

Man was able to, for a moment, to see beyond the physical reality that he was part of, he was able to think abstractly. This occurred precisely when, by accident, the conflict of all-against-all turned to a conflict between all-against-one. The first scapegoat, according to Girard, was the birthplace of language and consequently, society. The survivors of the conflict realized that when the scapegoat was murdered, there was momentary peace in the community.

When this phenomenon was repeated across time, it became embedded as an abstract symbol. And because it was a symbol that represented a momentary break from conflict, it became sacred. This first symbol was the cause of man's cognitive development, and eventually, because man became capable of abstraction, language was possible, and this led to the creation of society.

In summary, mimesis led to scapegoating which then led to the first sacred symbol which developed the first instance of language. This culminated in the first ritual which eventually resulted in religion which finally culminated in culture.

That is a very rough sketch of "mimetic theory" as it pertains to the origin of society. But the other part of mimetic theory is what happens after the founding of society. And according to Girard, the social mechanism that led to momentary peace, the scapegoat, was in fact, based on a lie. It was based on the presumed guilt of the victim. The victim was not always guilty.

For the scapegoat mechanism to work, all members of the community must believe that the victim is indeed guilty (méconnaissance). And when the victim is killed, scapegoated, then the perception is that the evil in the community has been purged. And this brings peace, but the peace will only last until conflict once again arises.

This phenomenon became inscribed in mythology and was celebrated. Using ancient texts such as Sophocles (Oedipus the king), Girard demonstrated that sacred and archaic religion is based on the scapegoat mechanism.

A crucial point should be made. It is not that Girard was saying that all myths included the scapegoat, but that of the myths that did include the scapegoat, they all shared a common feature, and that was the belief that the scapegoat was indeed guilty. This continued for millennia, until it was interrupted by the Judeo-Christian religion. The Christian story subverted the mythological mechanism by diffusing its most important feature (the unawareness of the perpetrators with regards to the innocence of the victim).

At the heart *of I See Satan Fall Like Lightning*, a book Girard published in 1999, one finds a comparative analysis of religious myths and Judeo-Christian revelation. In Girard's eyes, it is precisely the difference between these two forms of religion that displays the truth of

Christianity. In Genesis, the failure to sacrifice Isaac was the first interruption of the sacrificial pattern. And in *Rene Girard's Mimetic Theory*, Palazer cites numerous examples from the Bible, such as the Book of Job, Cain and Abel, King Solomon and the Two Harlots, and the story of Jesus Christ, to show that in each case, there was a clear rejection of mimesis. There was a rejection both of scapegoating and of man's imitation of man. This was a clear contrast to other anthropologists who viewed Judaism and Christianity as a continuation of the tradition of sacrifice.

Since Girard was originally a secular literary scholar, before he became a Christian, his discovery of mimesis came from literary works, and these are also cited in the book.

From the beginning, René Girard's mimetic theory was independent of the influence of traditional theories of secularization. This was because he was more interested in theoretical approaches that assumed a maverick role regarding the question of religion and, in great contrast to the secularist theories dominating the humanities, did not foresee any impending end to religion.

Close Conflict

In people who are closer, such as siblings, the desire to be unique from each other is dominant. But both are alike in that they both want to stand apart. They are more alike that they are comfortable admitting to themselves.

Recall that the narcissism of small differences is the thesis that communities with adjoining territories and close relationships are especially likely to engage in feuds and mutual ridicule because of hypersensitivity to details of differentiation.

Enzensberger, the German author, notes that "it is generally the rule, rather than the exception, that man destroys what he most hates, and that is usually the rival on his own territory. There is an unexplained linkage between hating one's neighbor and hating a stranger. The original target of our hatred was probably always our neighbor; only with the formation of larger communities was the stranger on the other side of the border declared an enemy."

Like Girard, who refers to man's "centripetal tendency" for violence, the German author says that violence within the group precedes external violence. The cultivated wars between nations are an explicitly recent development.

And herein is an apparent paradox. If a belief in God brings harmony to people, then why do groups fight? A first candidate is Freud's narcissism of small differences. Because these groups are similar in so many ways, the small differences are exaggerated to the point that they become sources of conflict.

Freud criticized the communist belief that people are good by nature and the creation of property has corrupted them. Freud maintained that aggressive people have always existed, even in primitive times, and property has served as outlet for aggression to manifest itself. When very similar nations such as Spain and Portugal show their hatred to one another – what Freud called "the narcissism of minor differences" – we see another example of aggressive instincts being satisfied.

But Girard's mimetic theory would explain this differently. It is not simply the existence of small differences, but the existence of similarities that is the culprit. Because these people have much that is in common, they fight.

There is a confusion between who the emulator is, and who the model is. In hierarchical systems (within a religion), this conflict is lacking, but when two separate authorities that are similar in most ways (Catholics versus Protestants or Sunnis versus Shiites), it is not clear who should be following the other, or who should command more power, resources, or people. Civil wars between rival groups in the same country are more frequent and lengthier but less intense than wars between different countries.

That is why conflict is most common in nuclear families where the relationships are closest. Two siblings exist in almost the same reality. They have the same parents and have been exposed to many of the same things. They share the same genes, amplitudes, and they probably look alike. But the hierarchy is not always obvious. Knowing this, siblings strive to be different from each other, but ironically, their efforts at standing apart from the other makes them even more alike.

Mediation is external when the mediator of the desire is socially beyond the reach of the subject or, for example, a fictional character, as in the case of Amadis de Gaula and Don Quixote. The hero lives a kind of folly that nonetheless remains optimistic. Mediation is internal when the mediator is at the same level as the subject. The mediator then transforms into a rival and an obstacle to the acquisition of the object, whose value increases as the rivalry grows. This is the universe of the novels of Stendhal, Flaubert, Proust and Dostoevsky, which are particularly studied in this book.

Rene Girard's Mimetic Theory,
Wolfgang Palaver

Thus, mimesis is resolved through hierarchies. When there is possibility for competition, when one side is clearly superior to the other side, then rivalry does not exist, and so, conflict does not exist. It is only when the metaphorical distance between the subject and the model is minimal that rivalry intensifies, and conflict becomes inevitable.

The Mimetic Taboo

In culture, there is a taboo against mimesis. We praise originality and shun copycats and emulators. We refuse to admit our mimetic nature. But according to Girard, man lacks being, he feels intrinsically empty – this is a similar idea to Kierkegaard's man who is doomed to a life of anxiety.

The solution, the one most available to man is to adopt the desires of the group, to model himself after what other people value. But once this is accomplished, his desires become a source of conflict. While there is truth to this idea, one can object that it is not clear when such desires are indeed because of imitation, or because of hidden biological needs, or evolutionary imperatives that give man an advantage in surviving.

Anti-Mimetic Mimesis of Advertising

No other phenomenon displays the workings of mimetic desire more clearly than modern advertising. In commercials, we don't see the advertised object on the screen by itself – it is accompanied by people who possess and desire the object, to activate the viewer's imitation. Advertising is a "phenomenon of envy" according to German psychologist Rolf Haubl, who unknowingly alludes to mimetic theory, although he is unfamiliar with it.

"The economies of developed
consumer societies are not
faced with the task of
eliminating shortages, but
rather—in a world of
superabundance—of creating
them. Advertising is the portal
through which these shortages
are communicated. One
strategy of creating shortages
consists of making consumers
envious: they should desire the
goods that the models on
billboards and commercials
already possess."

Rolf Haubl

The athlete or actor on the poster holding the
drink/perfume/sunglasses, is the 'model' holding
an object. If you want to be like this athlete or
actor, then you must desire this drink or
sunglasses, which they also desire. In the
triangular model, you are the 'subject', the drink,
or sunglasses the 'object', and the athlete or
actor the 'mediator' or 'model.'

It is obvious that advertising is a mimetic
phenomenon. Girard goes further and elucidates

its paradoxical nature: although advertising presupposes mimetic desire, it must promote the anti-mimetic modern message (be original). Advertising promises originality, by promising the customer that they will become exceptionally unique, and differentiated from the mundane horde, once they own the product that is advertised by models.

But this promise is contradictory since imitation and original desire are mutually exclusive.

Fashion, for example, is clearly an ideal that is based on imitation. And the paradoxical nature of fashion is apparent: everyone wants to be unique in the way that they dress, but they do so by copying the inventions of other people.

The human being has a natural tendency to compare his behavior to that of a more important person (the child with adults, the lower-ranking person with those of higher rank) in order to imitate the other person's ways. A law of this imitation, which aims at not appearing lower than others, especially in cases where no regard to utility is paid, is called fashion. Fashion therefore belongs under the title of vanity,

because there is no inner worth
in its intention; and also of
foolishness, because in fashion
there is still a compulsion to let
ourselves be led slavishly by the
mere example that many in
society give us.

Immanuel Kant

Objections to Mimetic Theory

There are other desires, one could argue, such as the need for security, popularity, status, power– that are not based on imitation, only, but are necessary for survival in one way or another. Even fashion, it can be argued, aids in sexual selection and the multiplication of genes.

But such an objection does not invalidate mimetic theory, because what we clearly see around us, is not uniformity in terms of what people desire. If everyone was motivated purely by biological necessity or by innate personally quirks, we should not expect to find that culture makes any difference at all to what the individual within that culture desires.

What we see, as outlined in Huntington's famous work, *The Clash of Civilizations*, is that there are multiple civilizations that exist in the world (not the same as countries). The Chinese, Western, and Muslim civilizations each have their own hierarchical systems that determine what is most valuable and what is least valuable.

People who belong to these different civilizations desire different things, they have different values. They are dominated by different memes (ideas). The idea of a meme is a Self-organizing cluster of ideas. Huntington's thesis can also be interpreted in a different way, perhaps more obvious. It is not similarities (as Girard would argue) that brings rise to conflict, but rather the differences between people. But such an objection could be reconciled if we think about the idea of internal and external mediation.

The clash between civilizations occurs, because on the grand geopolitical stage, there is no longer external mediation, but only internal mediation. External mediation, when the model is outside your social (and competitive) sphere, is not a cause of conflict because as a subject, you have no way of competing for the same resources.

You occupy a different world, where only metaphysical imitation is possible, but acquisition at the expense of your model is not possible.

This picture radically changes when we have internal mediation. Here, the subject and the model occupy the same world (close conflict), and zero-sum games become possible. That is why, on the grand geopolitical stage, civilizations can conflict with each other – each civilization sees, as their natural right, to be the dominant civilization. But not all civilizations do this.

The civilizations that clash are the civilizations that have a claim to power. It is rare (or impossible) to see a clash of civilizations where one is vastly superior to the other.

Another objection is that divinity is not necessary, even if we grant that Christianity subverted the scapegoating mechanism.

What about free will? If human behavior is mimetic, and all desires are the result of a mimetic mechanism that is biologically programmed, then what choices are truly available? Can we choose from an infinite number which desires of models are worth emulating, or are these desires pre-determined by the availability of a limited number of models?

Girard would here invoke the idea of faith in God. Since external human models worth emulating determine some of the desires of most people, and internal human models determine some of the desires of each person, then desires based on other people cannot possibly be original or free. The only free choice is to imitate God. And this is an interesting argument – the perception of a belief in God is generally seen as opposed to the idea of free will since such a belief would reduce one's options. But the alternative to God is the human ideal (which is a result of mimesis) – thus man is left with the choice to worship God or a lesser god (human ideals) but cannot choose to worship nothing at all.

In some cultures, honor is more sought after than other cultures, while in other cultures, it is wealth or piety or popularity or prestige that is most valuable. Memes, although not articulated by Girard, is perhaps a subset of mimesis. We want what our model wants, but the meme itself is what drives our model's behavior, so it is what drives all behavior.

But these memes are essentially products of language – if they cannot be articulated, then they will cease to exist. And since language is a by-product of mimesis, then memes are a by-product of mimesis.

As discussed before, the competing theories behind human motivation take the form of either sex, power, or mimesis. But one must ask the question: are they mutually exclusive? Can power not be a disguised drive that ultimately leads to procreation? And can mimetics not be the mediator between the two, in that the will to power, or the urge to procreate are different forms of mimetics, that we emulate each other's sexual and power desires?

Such a synthesis would resolve the conflict between Girard and Freud, and Nietzsche. But such a resolution may not be possible after-all. If Girard is right, then sex and power are nested within mimetic theory, but sex and power would not be primary, which undermines the Nietzschean and Freudian arguments.

For "Mimetic Theory" to be true, we would have to witness forms of emulation that are universal and have nothing to do with power or sex. One such form, which is mentioned in *Rene Girard's Mimetic Theory*, is snobbery. Another is religious life. The Buddhist monk, for example, who lives a modest life where he exercises no power over others and does not marry, cannot be said to be motivated by either power or sex.

Further, the artist or writer who desires to be anonymous, and whose work is only discovered after they are dead, does not seem to be motivated by power or sex. But mimesis can explain these seemingly paradoxical natures of people. It is possible for the monk to be motivated by the desire for nirvana, which was inspired by his teacher (or to attain the prestige of his teacher), and for the artist to be driven by an innate urge for private Self-expression, or by beauty, or by the emulation of a hero (famous artist).

The psychoanalyst Carl Jung would agree with Girard on the point that sexuality and power are not primary. Jung's falling out with his mentor, Freud, was precisely about this very point. Jung saw no convincing evidence that sex was behind all human activity, he identified different agents within the unconscious that desire different things, and these archetypes are not all interested in power or sex.

The Desire for Being

But doesn't this just mean that people have different desires because they have different personalities or upbringings or genetic predispositions? Even if we grant that power and sex are not the ideals that animate the behavior of people, it could simply be that that some desires are shared because the personalities of people fall into universal categories, and it is not that desires result from models that are being imitated, but by a personality quirk that leads someone to gravitate to some things more than others.

And to that objection, I believe Girard would cite writers such as Proust, Dostoevsky, and Flaubert, that show through the characters of their novels, that personalities themselves are products of mimetic behavior.

The waiter acts in such a way, with a pattern of motion, speed, and attitude stimulate the model of 'waiter' in his mind, he is copying an ideal that he finds more security in than his improvisation. He is acting out a character, as observed by Sartre. The man who feels that a woman is attractive because others find her attractive, or because a role model of theirs finds her attractive.

Extent & Intensity

Girard says that desire is an intersubjective by-product. We want what we do only because other people desire it. We want fame because others want fame – the extent to which this desire is powerful, is dependent on who we are surrounded by. The answer to the objection, as mentioned before, to Girard's theory (the objection is that some desires are hidden but innate and are not based on imitation) is that we can see how cultures vary to the intensity with which some desires are experienced, the extent to which individuals of this culture share these desires, and the hierarchy of the objects that are desired.

Of course, there exists a difference of opportunities between nations. Perhaps a Tibetan and a New Yorker are equally driven by material wealth, but the desire is only more apparent in the New Yorker because they have more access to opportunities, but this does not negate the fact that cultures do not have the same priorities. Countries and civilizations that share the same degree of economic opportunities and wealth may still differ in their attitudes towards it.

The Buddhist in Tibet does not only shun possessions because of a lack of opportunities compared to the banker on Wall Street, but because of ideological differences. Girard would argue that this difference exists because each have different models that they are imitating. Since it is possible for an American or a European to decide to reject these opportunities because they are attracted to the Buddhist model, it is not merely the existence of opportunities that determines the level or type of desire.

And this is a consequence of globalization. It would have been true to say, that in the past, memes that individuals adopted were passed down from their own cultures, but now this is only partially true. And just as Mimetic Theory would predict, the internet has closed the gap between existing memes so that it is possible for a teenager in the Middle East to adopt Western memes, or for a Western teenager to adopt Buddhist memes. So that now, as part of the fourth-generation warfare that is taking place, the war of civilizational memes, through the mechanism of the internet and global media channels, has created a new kind of conflict that is much more democratized and much less controllable.

The Development of Language

And now we go to the beginning. After explaining what mimesis is, the competing theories for human motivation, we will now turn to an explanation for why language, which made memes and thus mimetics possible, came to being.

The first development of language, according to some is Machiavellianism. People had to develop sophisticated ways of outcompeting their rivals, and this increased neural complexity, which led to the development of language.

But the theory that hominization occurred because of the development of language begs the question, why humans? The theory that Machiavellianism evolved in humans, does not explain the bigger brains of humans. Chimps engage in Machiavellianism but have not developed anything close to human language. Further, why would it have developed in humans in the way that it did, even if Machiavellianism played a part?

Machiavellianism fails as an explanation because it begs the question. Why in humans and not in chimps?

But Girard argues that language developed from countless observations of the scapegoating process.

Primordial men imitated the desires of each other, but the objects of their desire were scarce, so this created conflict, and lead to a situation of all against all. This must have gone on for a very long time, until a development happened that made the resolution of conflict much more economical. The death of a single victim rather than mutual destruction of the tribes, created a moment of temporary peace. This temporary peace which interrupted conflict was etched into the minds of the survivors as a symbol (the first instance of symbolic language).

Thus, the process of scapegoating resolved dispute, brought peace, and was observed intensely. It was the first non-instinctual observation, the first instance of language (symbol representing something outside of itself), and this process continued for millennia. The scapegoat was a symbol for momentary peace. And from this process, our brains evolved.

Why did man, and not some other animal, develop this tendency to scapegoat, and to watch repeated rituals of this scapegoating process? Because man is the most imitative animal, by far. That is Girard's foundational thesis and is an Aristotelian observation.

Each human is mimetic. But because it is necessary does not mean it is not a problem. Usually, when we think of mimesis, we recall the image of cultural institutions, in that humans are taught to imitate the work of other human beings, but there is nothing to stop mimesis itself from being nefarious and acquisitive. Envy, for example, is the closest Christian sin to mimetic rivalry and remains a taboo even among postmodernists.

Girard thinks the social contract is an Enlightenment lie and a preposterous one. When you imagine how primitive man lived, in his vicious and barbaric state, where all was pitted against all, it is difficult to imagine that on a whim, they suddenly agreed to calm down for a few hours, and negotiate a social contract.

The Origin of Political and Religious Institutions

A more likely scenario, as mentioned above, is that this war of all against all persists with no rational stopping point, until one person becomes the scapegoat. The death of this person unites the community and brings limited peace to the survivors.

This murder is the secret origin of religious and political institutions, remembered as myth. But this violence which is at the heart of society had to be concealed by the myth that the slain victim was truly guilty.

Violence is at the heart of society, myth a discourse ephemeral to violence. Myth makes this violence sacred. Sacrifice thus became sacred, and anyone who rejected it, sacrilegious. But now, the cat is out of the bag. The scapegoat is not as guilty. But for society to function, there had to be a lack of understanding of this basic truth. In the modern world, this no longer works.

The Straussian Moment

In other words, the power of the myth no longer holds sway because its mechanism has been uncovered. We now know that the scapegoat is not as guilty, we understood the victimhood of the scapegoat in many cases is there, and this creates a barrier to normal functioning of the myth.

As Peter Thiel, an admirer of Girard says, the problem of mimesis, has not gone away. One can easily imagine a nuclear arms race that stems from mimesis. Not enough people are aware of the mimetic mechanism, although it seems that sufficient people are aware of the scapegoating mechanism.

In short, society understands the error in persecuting the innocent (yet scapegoating persists) but does not yet understand the origin of why this persecution arose, and that is mimesis (imitation of the desire of others).

Uncovering the Scapegoat Mechanism

The scapegoat can be internal (someone in the culture) or external (when one nation may go to war). Once you begin to grasp it, you see it everywhere. Mythology is different from the myth of the Bible, according to Girard, in contrast to conventional readings of mythology.

In the Bible, the sacrifice of Jesus is not a victory for the community, not a continuity of a past tradition, not a celebration of scapegoating. It is the opposite. It is the condemnation of the scapegoat mechanism, and the condemnation of mimesis itself. It is the unveiling of the innocent victim.

As we discussed before, the tendency for people to project evil onto others is the phenomenon of the shadow, which Jung wrote about.

Instead of taking responsibility for our shadow "we prefer to localize the evil with individual criminals or groups of criminals, while washing our hands in innocence and ignoring the general proclivity to evil. This sanctimoniousness cannot be kept up, in the long run, because the evil, as experience shows, lies in man – unless, in accordance with the Christian view, one is willing to postulate a metaphysical principle of evil. The great advantage of this *view is that it exonerates man's conscience of too heavy a responsibility and fobs it off on the devil, in correct psychological appreciation of the fact that man is much more the victim of his psychic constitution than its inventor."*

The Undiscovered Self, Carl Jung

Jung leaves us with some important questions to ponder about the perils brought about by the age of scientific rationalism, and the rejection of the Western Christian myth.

"So much is at stake and so much depends on the psychological constitution of modern man. Is he capable of resisting the temptation to use his power for the purpose of staging a world conflagration? Is he conscious of the path he is treading, and what the conclusions are that must be drawn from the present world situation and his own psychic situation? Does he know that he is on the point of losing the life

preserving myth of the inner man which Christianity has treasured up for him? Does he realize what lies in store should this catastrophe ever befall him? Is he even capable at all of realizing that this would be a catastrophe? And finally, does the individual know that he is the makeweight that tips the scales?"

Jung

When Jung wrote about the shadow; he was referring to the externalization of evil. Imagine a society with corrupt leaders who steal and pillage their way to power. They bribe their electorate, the state's security forces, and monopolize various industries. But they refuse to pass reforms, to avoid waste and corruption, and to act transparently. Yet come election season, and lo and behold, they are re-elected because they have done just enough to maintain their influence. In this fictional developing country, they are heroes.

And then, the country goes through a difficult economic period, and everything falls apart. The people who live within this dysfunctional democracy will not feel responsible. They will point the finger at the politicians and hold them accountable for the tragedy that they are going through. Only a small number will be brave enough to acknowledge that they have been complicit in all this. It is their fault for not speaking up, for voting for the wrong people, and for encouraging a corrupt system to grow and thrive. Jung's warning is a prophetic message for the ages, and for all people.

Before externalizing blame when things fall apart, whether it is your nation or a business venture that has failed, make sure that you are sufficiently Self-critical. So that at the very least, when things fall apart, you know that you deserve some of the blame. The alternative is to scapegoat the other group, to actively separate the wrongdoer from the group, and thus, to fall into the mimetic trap.

As Watts noted, Jung understood the polarity of life. He understood that there was harmonization between light and darkness, good and evil. Jung recognized that the proclivity for evil was just as human and universal as the proclivity for good. And it is this recognition that will allow people to resist the temptation to simplistically frame reality as consisting of good versus bad. Unfortunately, political discourse often takes this form.

The main task of the psychotherapist is to do what is called, 'to integrate the evil.' To, as it were, put the devil in us in its proper function. Because you see, it's always the devil, the unacknowledged one, the outcast, the scapegoat, the bastard, the bad guy, the black sheep of the family. It's always from that point that generation comes. In other words, in the same way as in the drama, to have the play, it's necessary to introduce the villain, to introduce a certain element of trouble. So, in the whole scheme of life, there has to be an element of the shadow, because without the shadow, there cannot be the substance.

– Alan Watts

Politicians, in general, do not behave as if they are aware of their shadow, they act as if they are leading the fight against tyranny and corruption, by reassuring their supporters of their pure intentions, and by weaving a comforting nationalistic narrative. If your country stands for liberty, freedom, and democracy – then it must be the case that those who act in the name of your country are acting according to these values! For all his faults, Jung embodied the "old wise man" and the "fool" archetypes. As Watts recalled, one of the wise and inconvenient truths that Jung understood and taught throughout his life was this: to the degree that you condemn others and find evil in them, you are to that degree unconscious to the same thing in yourSelf (or at least the potentiality of it).

"Do you believe," said Candide, "that men have always massacred each other as they do to-day, that they have always been liars, cheats, traitors, ingrates, brigands, idiots, thieves, scoundrels, gluttons, drunkards, misers, envious, ambitious, bloody-minded, calumniators, debauchees, fanatics, hypocrites, and fools?" "Do you believe," said Martin, "that hawks have always eaten pigeons when they have found them?" "Yes, without doubt," said Candide. "Well, then," said Martin, "if hawks have always had the same character why should you imagine that men may have changed theirs?"

Candide, Voltaire

The Wise King

In the Old Testament, there is story of King Solomon.

The story is that two harlots, alike in every way, were about to give birth, but one harlot, after she had discovered that her baby had died because she had smothered it, replaced her dead baby with the baby of the other harlot, which was alive. When both harlots appeared before the wise king, to resolve the conflict of who the rightful mother of the baby was, Solomon put them through a test.

He asked for a sword so that he would divide the baby in half and give each harlot half a baby. One of the Harlots, the rightful mother, yelled out in protest. She told King Solomon to give the baby to the other harlot, but not to kill the baby. That is when the wise king knew who the real mother was and ordered that the baby be given to her.

The harlot who did not object would have been perfectly happy to see the baby cut in half, for she did not want her rival to be better off. But the true mother risked everything.

She knew, before saying anything, that her cries of protest could easily be interpreted as an admission of her own guilt. After-all, the sight of a dead baby would be too unbearable for a lie to persist, which had now grown too large. She could not have known how King Solomon was going to interpret her actions, but she took the risk anyway, and in this sense, there is an element of Self-sacrifice.

That is the point that Girard makes in *Things Hidden Since The Foundation of The World*. The harlot engages in Self-sacrifice, but not in order to attain divinity. The Harlot did not know she was going to be rewarded with her baby after she sacrificed herself. And Jesus was not made immortal by the resurrection, he was already immortal, and the resurrection was just a consequence of that fact.

Whereas in mythology, the act of sacrifice is one where the hero, who is sacrificed is divinized. In fact, many practices that still survive, make this apparent. When the prisoner who is sentenced to death, for example, is given a last meal of his choosing and a glass of rum.

Past cultures treated sacrificial victims like Gods. In the archetypal myth, the sacrifice is what rescues the community. The scapegoat brings about temporary order and restores the peace. The scapegoat is glorified. Human mimesis is celebrated. Girard is saying that this is all in stark contrast to the message contained in the Bible.

Jesus explicitly denounces mimesis, the idea of coveting what one's neighbor is in possession of is considered morally wrong.

To live for the attainment of wealth or fame or pleasure, or for the satisfaction of any earthly desire is a sin, since they are the products of other men. These desires are products of mimesis.

The cyclical process of mimesis, conflict, and finally, sacrificial resolution through the scapegoat, is contradicted by the story of Jesus.

The end of the ritualistic scapegoating process that brought peace, came with Christianity, when this unconscious process was revealed, but came with it two important repercussions. The birth of freedom and responsibility, and the end of the soothing ritual of the scapegoating process.

Girard's ultimate solution to this problem is Christianity, which he believes precludes mimetic conflict, because instead of emulating a human model which may eventually be a rival, and thus a source of conflict, and instead of building a society of emulators of one another, which will eventuate in competition, which will create less opportunities for each individual, and inevitably result in conflict, one should emulate a divine model (also Kierkegaard's solution), to let go of our vanity and pride, and to accept our fate as creatures that have a creator.

It is specifically the imitation of Christ that Girard argues for since Christ is the anti-myth. Myths all share a common structure: there is a disruption of peace in the community, there is a scapegoat, the mob kills the scapegoat, peace is restored. In the story of Christ, the structure is opposed to the standard mythical narrative. Instead of being on the side of the mob, it stands on the side of the victim, Jesus. It is not only that Jesus preached against mimesis, but his actions advocated this counter-narrative directly. And so, we find in this counter-narrative, a pathway that leads to the end of violence, and the subversion of the devil (which Girard argues is the mimetic mechanism itself).

Why do men compete? Is it because of genetic programming that compels the individual to be selected, replicate and survive or do they compete out of vanity – out of a drive to accumulate what their model desires? Are men free to not compete, to counteract their own conditioning? If so, is this proof of free will?

There are other causes of desire that differ from mimesis (as Girard would accept), not all desires can be accounted for by the mimetic mechanism, but many can. Since we know that it is true that human beings are the most mimetic creature, we know that human beings must have the capacity for the highest forms of emulation and the lowest forms. But what is meaningful about Mimetic Theory? It is not that it accounts for all human desires, but that it proves that if we allow unconscious mimetic tendencies to take control of our decision making, we may find ourselves in the pursuit of goals that we do not value or need. And out of such a pursuit, we may find ourselves caught in the inevitable conflict that results.

It appears that there are two ways out of the mimetic trap. One is to externalize one's models. The further the model from one's immediate reality, the less the chance for a conflict of interests. A baker on a corner street in Rome is better off modeling a famous bakery in France than a famous bakery across the street. The other is to avoid blind the idealization of human pursuits.

Chapter 7: A Union of Opposites

Dichotomy 19: Beast vs God

The foundation of Kierkegaard's philosophy is the Fall in the story of Adam and Eve because it contains the basic insight of psychology, that man is a union of opposites – Self-consciousness and the physical body. The fall into consciousness from a carefree life came with a grave penalty: anxiety.

An animal or a "beast" cannot feel dread since they don't have a spirit or a "Self." If man was a beast or an angel, he would not experience dread, but it is his ambiguity that dooms him. Since he cannot reconcile his paradoxical nature, he cannot ignore his fate. At the same time, he cannot take control of it. But according to Ernest Becker, it is not the ambiguity itself that is the real cause of dread, but the judgment on man that if Adam eats of the fruit of the tree of knowledge God tells him "Thou shalt surely die." It is the knowledge of one's own mortality that is the ultimate terror of consciousness.

Kierkegaard describes the man who limits himself from possibility, a closed personality, and says that this type is the inauthentic man. He is the one who avoids developing his uniqueness, he follows uncritically the modes of living that he was taught as a child. This type of man is inauthentic because he does not belong to himself, he does not see reality for what it is - they are completely immersed in social games. This is the corporate man in the West, the bureaucrat in the East, and the man of tradition in the tribe, they shy away from the possibility of thinking for themselves. This is the immediate man.

The philistine (the immediate man) to Kierkegaard was the man who is lulled by simple pleasures – a city dweller in his time. In today's world, they content themselves by going to the mall or taking a two-week summer vacation. It is not that there is anything wrong with simple pleasures. Kierkegaard's point was that these simple pleasures were enough for such a person. Why would anyone want to live such a trivial life? Because there is great danger in the full horizon of experience.

Carl Jung once wrote, "beware of unearned wisdom." There is a danger to the attainment of knowledge that one is not ready for. Historically, only a minority of people dared to question the social order and seek their own answers. So, the individual that Kierkegaard is describing is the most common kind that exists, and that has always existed.

Kierkegaard thought that philistinism celebrates triumph over possibility and freedom. The real enemy is freedom because it threatens to pull you into a void, while giving it up too much would make you a prisoner of necessity. In other words, the unbridled pursuit of truth carries with it dire consequences, it can shake the foundations underneath an individual and throw them into an abyss. Practically, a devastating idea. But on the other hand, there is the opposite danger. The individual who refuses freedom altogether becomes limited, not fully human in a way. Kierkegaard understood that the safest path is the socially permissible one. Too much possibility can put you in a madhouse, and he recognized that psychosis is just neurosis taken to the extreme.

Dichotomy 20: The Possible vs The Impossible

And here we arrive at the ultimate dichotomy, according to Kierkegaard. The truth about man is that he has two natures. If he ignores the symbolic Self and the limitations of his finite body, then he will live a lie, fail to realize his own nature, and be "the most pitiful of all things."

The ideal man for Kierkegaard acted from a unified center, acknowledged one's dualism, understood one's own limitations, and combined it with possibility. The person that goes too extreme in exploring without limitations becomes schizophrenic, while the person is constantly chained by what is possible, and refuses to explore, becomes depressed. And the depressed person, because they cannot act or move or draw breath, appear dumb.

The two types of men are opposites. The immediate man lives for trivial things and distractions, which are enough to keep his mind away from existential dread, and Self-contradiction. He may lead a normal life, have a job, and a family, and he will hope for awards and victories, with the secret that only he knows, that he has no "Self."

Then, Kierkegaard describes the introvert, and he is someone who withdraws from the world, reflects on his true nature, and what unique talents he might have that he could offer the world, he is not like the immediate man, he cannot content himself with trivialities. Unlike immediate man, the connection to family, or his country's flag, are not enough for the introvert, since he feels within himself something deeper that has not yet been realized or discovered, but he does not always find it. For this reason, the introvert is described as a "real man" only in appearance, but not necessarily in reality.

Kierkegaard describes the introvert type who can lead a normal life, become a university professor and start a family, and have some quiet moments, and content himself with a feeling of slight superiority to others, but he will not go further, since he is afraid of where that may take him. But this is not a sustainable position, since Self-awareness even in small doses can get you in trouble. This person, if they are strong, may not be able to bear it, they may drown themselves into the world desperately in the rush of experience.

And then there is the final type of man.

The one who asserts himself out of defiance of his own weakness, who tries to be a god unto himself, the master of his fate, a Self-created man. He will not be merely the pawn of others, of society; he will not be a passive sufferer and secret dreamer, nursing his own inner flame in oblivion. He will plunge into life. into the distractions of great undertakings, he will become a restless spirit... which wants to forget…. Or he will seek forgetfulness in sensuality, perhaps in debauchery.

Fictitious Health

Kierkegaard did not claim to know what a healthy life was, but he knew that it had possibility and freedom, and he knew what it was not. It was not being a "normal cultural man" for this was a sign of sickness. There is such a thing as "fictitious health."

This idea was also recognized by Nietzsche. Mental health is not typical, it is ideal-typical. It is not in being oneself, but in overcoming oneself. The ideal man is something to be achieved. The healthy man, and the true man is the one who has transcended himself.

How does he transcend himself?

By recognizing the truth of his situation, by breaking away the lie of his character, and running free from his conditioned prison. Like Freud, the problem for Kierkegaard were the defenses that protect Self-esteem against terror. They are the very defenses that allow him to move forward in life with Self-confidence – these are his life-long trap.

Kierkegaard knew that it was difficult to break out of one's routines, to explore life with its possibilities and accidents and choices. In the prison of one's character one can pretend and feel that the world is manageable, that there is a reason for one's life. The truth of man's condition is that he is an animal, and this is where the anxiety comes from.

But this flood of anxiety is not the end, it is the school that provides man with the ultimate maturity. It is a better teacher than reality, because the latter can be twisted and distorted by culture, but the feeling of anxiety can never be a lie.

The curriculum in this school is the unlearning of repression, and this includes the fear of death. The key is to face one's own finitude.

Kierkegaard's whole argument now becomes crystal clear, as the keystone of faith crowns the structure. We can understand why anxiety "is the possibility of freedom," because anxiety demolishes "all finite aims," and so the "man who is educated by possibility is educated in accordance with his infinity." Possibility leads nowhere if it does not lead to faith.

The task of man should be to break free from the chains of the social fictions he has been indoctrinated with, and to go on a journey of Self-discovery. In this journey, he will encounter the feeling of dread, because of his dualistic and paradoxical situation, because of his finitude, and it is at this point that he must resist using character defenses that have worked for him in the social world. Once he has accepted this anxiety, he can allow himself to be open to possibility, and the destination for man is faith. The truly open person who has shed his character armor is beyond the help of "science" or any social standard of health.

He is alone, and on the brink of oblivion. Only faith can give him the support he needs, and the courage to renounce dread without any dread. This is not an easy way out, and not a solution for everyone, but since man is an ambiguous creature, he will always experience anxiety, he cannot get rid of it.

But he can use this anxiety as an eternal fountain that produces new dimensions of thought and trust. Faith poses a new life-task, the adventure in openness to a multi-dimensional reality.

4
THE DICHOTOMY OF SELF AND EGO

Chapter 8: The Ego Illusion

Self-Deception

"A man who lies to himself, and believes his own lies, becomes unable to recognize truth, either in himself or in anyone else, and he ends up losing respect for himself and for others. When he has no respect for anyone, he can no longer love, and in him, he yields to his impulses, indulges in the lowest form of pleasure, and behaves in the end like an animal in satisfying his vices. And it all comes from lying — to others and to yourSelf."

Fyodor Dostoevsky

The idea of deception is easy for most people to understand. It is not a puzzle that some people are able to deceive others. But why would anyone deceive themselves? Why would an intelligent being, engineered for survival, purposefully play a malicious trick on itself?

In *Self-Deception*, Herbert Fingarette insists that it is no paradox at all. He makes his argument by analyzing a few everyday experiences that anyone can relate to.

One such experience is writing in a crowded coffee shop. The sound of chatter and clattering should distract you, but if you are focused on writing, your mind ignores all extraneous noise.

This is made possible by your ability to ignore sounds that do not contribute to your mission. And then, imagine that a friend walks by while talking on the phone. You do not hesitate to turn around, because the voice you have heard is too familiar.

Because your mind can choose what to ignore, you can deceive yourSelf.

If you can selectively ignore input with ease, then you can ignore most of reality with ease. You can choose to believe the narratives and the facts that are most Self-serving and ignore the information that do not fit your story.

The ability to ignore what is not relevant, to engage in confirmation bias, is a symptom of the human capacity for Self-deception. And the polarization that exists in politics, academia, sports, and religion across the world is proof of the ubiquity of this capacity in people.

The psychological literature teaches us that we repress ideas and memories, and that we do so as a defense mechanism. Self-deception can sometimes be harmful but is necessary for a healthy psyche. If you repress shame after making a mistake, you would feel flustered if you were confronted about it, that is because you have not taken the time to think about your behavior, and to process it well.

You were taken off guard because you chose to ignore a part of reality, to be dishonest with yourSelf. Since a habit of dishonesty will carry with it negative future consequences, many years later, you will feel less integrated and confident – it is hard to trust yourSelf when you have proven yourSelf capable of slick Self-sabotage. But Self-sabotage in the long run, such as the repression of shame, was traded for less depression and stress in the short run.

Herbert's conclusion is that Self-deception is not a paradox, but a staple in human behavior, that it is necessary for psychological health and socialization. Yet, Dostoevsky warned us of taking Self-deception to an extreme, living too much in a comfortable lie, and the repercussions, particularly in the long term, that will result from it.

A trade-off between short-term psychic health, and long-term life quality, is a standard one, that each person makes with each decision they make.

Nietzsche alluded to this when he said that "The strength of a person's spirit would then be measured by how much 'truth' he could tolerate, or more precisely, to what extent he needs to have it diluted, disguised, sweetened, muted, falsified."

Why is the truth difficult to "handle"? Why is it a "bitter pill to swallow"? Why is it "inconvenient"?

Because the truth cuts through the tricks that your mind plays in the name of sound mental health. A lie is never inconvenient, it is instrumental. But the truth is an obstacle to your goals, it breaks down your defense mechanisms and collapses your sense of certainty. By pursuing it, you engage in a courageous battle with no certain outcomes, but this does not make the pursuit of truth a fruitless adventure, only an uncomfortable one, and oftentimes, an impractical one.

Again, we revert back to the Taoist principle of balance. The most reasonable conclusion would be to 'pursue as much truth as you can bear, but no more.'

What is the Self?

The first question to ask, if we are to understand human nature, is "what is the Self?" Where did this idea come from? And finally, is it true?

We take it for granted that we have a Self, and it is our responsibility to cultivate it. The Ancient Greeks demanded, "Know thySelf!" And modern philosophers, historians, and philosophers have echoed the same message. But we don't have a unified definition of the Self.

The "Self" as thought of in modern civilization is not the same as the "Self" which existed in an early era, or even the "Self" that exists in some remote parts of the world that have not modernized.

What is the Self? If it exists, why are there so many definitions?

The psychoanalyst Sigmund Freud has defined the Self as a collection of opposing drives (id, ego, supergo) or (eros, thanatos). Jung followed in his footsteps and found some more ways to split the Self: persona/shadow and anima/animus dichotomy, in addition to his idea of the true Self – that core part of the person that is an artifact of the collective unconscious. You are, on Jung's account, the genetic heritage of the ideas of your ancestors. Rene Girard, the French literary critic, concluded that you are essentially mimetic. You simply mimic the behavior of others. That is, your goals are merely borrowed from the desires of others. As you engage in mimesis, you enter in a conflict with our double – another dichotomy of selves.

The Eastern traditions, such as Buddhism, maintains that the Self as it is commonly defined in Western civilization, which consists of a narrative, desires, thoughts, and feelings, is simply an illusion. The belief is that the true Self exists as a subjective experiencer of present phenomena.

Christianity argues that the Self is split between the forces of good and evil, and that you live in a constant struggle between the two, but that you choose freely what you want to do. The other monotheistic religions, Judaism, and Islam, agree. This idea of an autonomous Self is the one that is commonly agreed upon in civilization. The judiciary system would have no reason to exist if agency was an illusion. There is an implicit belief that the individual can exercise their own choices with regards to moral dilemmas. And if they make the wrong choice, they ought to be punished for it.

But modern neuroscientists, like Sam Harris, have argued that your Self is an illusion and that you have no free will. Simple changes to the anatomy of your brain will change you how experience the world and what you think about it. The latest findings in gut science corroborates this idea. We now know that our thoughts and behavior may be influenced to a large degree by our gut biota, giving the phrase 'you are what you eat' an extra dimension of rigor. And then, if we add the other pieces of knowledge we have acquired, from evolutionary psychology and behaviorism, then it becomes difficult to locate a place in the discussion for an autonomous "Self". It seems that all that we are lacking to collectively agree that the individual is not free is more precise data, which will inevitably come.

But is it true than humans are not freer than animals?

The Dissolution of the Ego

Starting in the 1950s, Buddhism recognized something like what psychologists labelled a "sense of Self." This was shortened to "Self" as if there was a real Self that exists somewhere inside of us. But intuitively, we have a notion about what it feels like to be us. I know that I can move my arm or leg, and it is my mind that is issuing the command. So, it is obvious that I at least have a sense of Self – a sense of agency with regards to the physical movements I choose to make.

Beyond this simplistic and unproblematic definition of the Self, which only considers a sense of direct agency with regards to physical movements, the individual adopts a much more sophisticated set of ideas about the Self, and these include ideas about the jobs or careers the individual was born to do, the political position they associate with, and the genres of music they find most pleasurable to listen to. These, along with many other ways the individual relates to the world, are recognized as the Self.

All these ideas can only exist because of society. Without society, there is no "Self" as it has just been defined. So, the Self is not innate, it is interpersonal. The Self can only exist in relation to others.

Dichotomy 21: Self vs Ego

According to Buddhism, these ideas of the Self, accultured by society, are a great source of suffering. Buddhism does not recognize a Self or ego. The idea that we have a Self is merely a mistake, so there is nothing to destroy of get rid of.

Through close observation, we can become aware that the idea "I am a separate Self" is false, and we let go of it. But doing this verbally or rationally is useless. The error must be corrected deep in the unconscious, where the false concept of the Self originates.

The word "ego" typically means a person's sense of Self-esteem or Self-awareness. Freud thought that the ego was a part of the mind that mediated between the conscious and the unconscious and is responsible for reality testing and creating a sense of personal identity.

A familiar idea, that originated in the East, is the dissolution of the ego. This line of thought obliterates the sense of separation that we see in the world. The well-known trope, usually associated with heavy use of psychedelics or psychoactive drugs, is that 'everything is connected'. And if that is true, then on some level, this means that labels and formal schooling has created a distinction between individuals. This distinction may be functional and real, but as McGilchrist points out, there is a difference between separation and distinction.

You can be distinct but not separate. For example, you are distinct from the person you were ten years ago, but you have never separated from that person. There are many ways in which we practically benefit from classifying the world into its component parts, and measuring these parts, but it is essentially our attempt to control nature. When the world is broken down into its component parts, then you can better understand how it works, and therefore, you can be more effective in manipulating it. But to be adept at manipulating the world does not necessarily mean that you understand the mechanisms behind it, nor does it mean that you are separate from it. The point that Bernardo Kastrup makes is that we have mistaken the interface for objective reality.

Kastrup, a Dutch computer scientist and philosopher, thought that we have made a fundamental mistake in trying to understand the world. We are essentially fed a materialist worldview the moment we begin our formal education. But this worldview is contradicted by recent scientific discoveries. The materialist worldview advances the idea that everything is made up of matter. And the mind is just an offspring of inanimate matter. Kastrup turns this idea on its head, returning to the old idealists (Berkeley) and says, no, the world is made up of consciousness. The only thing we know for sure is that we have a subjective experience of reality, and yet somehow, the materialist worldview has gone so far as to even deny that, by saying the consciousness is an illusion.

Returning to the idea about the dissolution of the ego, the point the Eastern mystics made was that there is no ego, it is all an illusion. Notice the difference between this perspective and materialism. One perspective says that the ego is an illusion, that since our thoughts are beyond our voluntary control, they cannot really be who we are. The only thing that is real for sure is consciousness. That is what Kastrup is saying.

But the materialist perspective goes the other way and says that consciousness is the illusion. The only thing that really exists is physical matter. Philosophers like Daniel Dennet have advanced this line of reasoning.

I will not discuss which of these ideas are right. But notice the dichotomy in perspectives here. It's as if one side is using their right brain while the other is using their left.

What is the Eastern perspective on the ego? As time passes, whether it is a moment or a year, our thoughts change, our priorities shift, and our identity morphs into something totally new and alien to what it once was. Since nothing, including our identity or future, is within our control, then we have crafted a masterful illusion for ourselves by identifying ourselves with a fixed Self, and this illusion is an endless source of misery and frustration.

That is why the Buddhistic solution is to cut off the ego, to let go of the personal narrative that we have built in our lives, and simply be present, and become aware of the wholeness of nature, and the fact that there is no difference between you and everything else.

Many authors have tried to popular this idea in the Western world, including Carl Jung, and Alan Watts. We will discuss some of their ideas in this book, but a more recent popularizer of the

Eastern perspective was Eckhart Tolle, who wrote *The Power of Now* in 1997.

But what does it mean to say that there is no separation between yourSelf and everything else in the world? You rarely think that there is no distinction between yourSelf and others/nature when someone cuts you off on the highway, or when you catch the flu and stay in bed for a week or when you need to pay for the bill at the end of the meal at a restaurant. If everything is so connected, then why does it feel like there world is made up of separate agents, each working towards their Self-interest, often at your expense?

The experience of "I" as something clearly distinct and separate is not just taken for granted, but it is the entire purpose of life. Without a personal narrative, what does the individual strive towards? What meaningful goals can be accomplished?

It is these kinds of concerns that prevent most people in modern economies from embracing the right-brained way of thinking. Like it or not, reality exists, and totally living in the present at the expense of planning for the future is bound to have severe repercussions to one's life. There is a practical world that cannot be ignored. Besides, isn't the ultimate adventure, the construction of the ego, a process that unfolds gradually, the entire purpose of life?

But to be fair to the right-brained perspective, which is making a moralistic, spiritual, and psychological point, it is not calling for a total elimination of the ego – a task that is not possible. The point is to weaken the identification with the ego. In the same way that Buddhistic teachings don't call for the elimination of pleasure, but for the elimination of the attachment to pleasure.

Likewise, McGilchrist didn't recommend a total renunciation of the left-brain, that would only result in another imbalance. The point is to correct for the left-brain bias that currently exists.

Philip Zimbardo, the psychologist who was involved in the famous Stanford prison experiments wrote a book called *The Time Paradox*.

He lists six different time perspectives we might have.

Past-positive and past-negative are positive and negative ways of perceiving past events. Present-hedonist means you live for the moment, experiencing as much pleasure as possible. Present-fatalist means you're anxious about the present because you feel your fate has been determined, and it is not favorable. A future-orientation involves a focus planning and preparing. And a transcendental future attitude means you believe in a life beyond physical death.

Eckhart Tolle spent two years sleeping on park benches before writing his book, *The Power of Now*. During that time, he could aptly be described as present-oriented – as the book title might suggest. But, unlike the dichotomy between pleasure and anxiety that Zimbardo suggests, Tolle existed in a meditative state, experiencing joy rather than pleasure. Joy is an experience that is experienced internally while pleasure can be induced by an external stimulus. Tolle could also be described as someone with a transcendental future orientation.

Most people would complain that they do not have the time to do what Tolle did. That is, to bask in the sun, and experience eternal oneness without a thought about tomorrow, while sleeping on random benches. They have responsibilities, deadlines, and constraints. But again, like McGilchist, Tolle called for balance, and not a total abandonment of future responsibilities.

Tolle delineated between two types of time. The 'constant living in the future or ruminating about the past' was what Tolle called psychological time, in contrast to clock time. Clock time consists in planning for the future, being diligent, having a schedule, and carefully reviewing the details and learning from your mistakes. Psychological time consists of ruminating on past experiences and living with a constant feeling of dread or anxiety. Tolle's point was to learn to stop incurring psychological time.

In *The Art of Living,* Goenka, an Indian teacher of Vipassana meditation, makes a similar point. People who have not meditated or read the literature on meditation think that it promotes a passive, lazy, and unproductive lifestyle.

But this is a misconception. It is the opposite. Practicing meditation (Vipassana in this book) is a difficult and effortful exercise that helps you focus on the present and ignore distracting thoughts about the past and the future.

It is necessary to plan, and important to reminisce, but doing this all the time is counterproductive. Unfortunately, the default state of our minds is to think about the past and future.

It is not that future concerns are irrelevant and should not be catered to, but an unhealthy obsession with the future can get in the way of your ability to think clearly about how you should live in the present. More than that, it robs you of the ability to live in the present.

Goenka taught that if you refuse to live in the moment, then you will never be able to achieve equanimity (or balance).

If you want to be free, there are two ways of doing it. The first is to gain equanimity. The second is the understand that your thoughts are transient. Neither condition is enough on its own. If you do both successfully, then you can cut off the sources of your misery, which will enable you to break free from the negative conditioning of the past.

The problem is that if you only learn equanimity, that is, to silence your inner urges, then you are merely suppressing your impulses temporarily. But you will not get rid of them, and you do not cut off their source.

You may appear calm, but underneath, there is a flurry of unconscious activity that is waiting to explode. The Buddha had this insight long before the invention of psychoanalysis. He understood that there was such a thing as the unconscious, and that thoughts that are repressed do not go away.

On the other hand, if you only understand the transient nature of your thoughts intellectually, without learning how to maintain balance, then you will continue to suffer, and to be pulled in different directions by immediate sensations and urges.

Intellectual liberation, or Vipassana, requires you to pass through multiple stages. And this includes a practice that existed before the Buddha. You must learn to focus on your breaths and physical sensations before you learn to meditate on your thoughts.

One of the ephemeral sensations you feel is pain. If you focus, you will notice that pain ebbs and flows – it is not constant. And like everything in nature, it will pass. Your body will always call to your attention the most urgent thing. If you are overly sensitive to each sensation, then you will feel debilitated.

Meditation will help you observe pain for what it is, and this will make you more immune to its effects. You will be better prepared to enduring feelings of displeasure or discomfort.

Through Vipassana, you will gain insight into yourSelf, and into the irrational attachments that you have. Each person is conditioned to be addicted to various things – whether social acceptance or admiration, physical pleasure, or intoxication.

Vipassana is a practice that can lead you outside your past conditioning. The past consists of choices that you have made, inadvertently in many cases, that have strengthened a certain kind of mental programming. Meditation is a way to de-program your mind, to cut away the parts and bits that are unnecessary or detrimental.

This does not mean that you will be free from desire, but that you will be more deliberate and in control of the things that you choose to desire.

Jung didn't think introversion was as bad but did think that one-sided introversion was detrimental to psychic health. He thought that both introversion and extroversion were necessary even though it is natural for one side to be dominant. Jung saw a resemblance between modern spontaneous dreams and ancient myths, their motifs were eerily similar. This led him to postulate that there had to be some innate human capacity to produce parallel images and ideas – those structures of the psyche are what he later called the 'archetypes of the collective unconscious.'

In addition to the ego, which organized and deliberated, there was a hidden unconscious center in the psyche, and this was what he called the 'Self' – in contrast to the ego. While we think we know ourselves, we are sometimes puzzling to ourselves. What you know about yourSelf is never the complete picture. The Self is the part of you that you try to discover – hence 'Self-realization.'

Jung was interested in the struggle between the ego and the Self, and how the ego attains the experience of supraordinate Self. But the process of development of the ego-consciousness and the way in which the Self guides the maturation of the ego are topics not covered by Jung, but by two Jungian analysts, Erich Neumann and Michael Fordham.

Neumann says that the child initially conceives of himself of being one with his mother, and only later discovers that he is a separate entity. That is the beginning of autonomy and the foundation of the ego. He coined the term 'ego-Self axis' to describe the relationship between the total Self and the ego – sometimes they move in the same direction, other times, in opposite directions.

The child feels a sense of disconnection from the world only later. The reason why children are so narcissistic, as I will later explain, is that they do not separate between the world and themselves. To them, they are one and the same. This sense of fundamental connectedness is eventually lost. As the individual becomes an adult, an accumulation of civilizational forces and the development of the intellect contribute to the individual's feeling of isolation.

To recap, a potential antidote to the conflict between the individual and the group is sublimation. But there are other conflicts. In *The Undiscovered Self,* Jung argues that the world is prevented from disintegrating into chaos by a stable minority of individuals. The masses are not responsible for order, because they drown out reason and individuality, they are the prelude to tyranny. The would-be tyrants are psychopaths who bring out to the surface the repressed elements of the masses, but these future tyrants, while a minority, are hard to detect and are extremely dangerous.

Jung tells us that our Self-knowledge is an offshoot of what our immediate social environment believes it knows about itself. But true Self-knowledge can only occur after assessing individual facts about oneself – which is why general theories are poor devices. For example, you might have read some statistics, and know about averages, but theories that tell you about the average are not telling you very much about yourSelf. Absolute reality "has the character of irregularity."

What is Jung talking about exactly? Think about averages and statistical facts that are presented to you every day. They constitute a form of knowledge. But this knowledge is not the same as understanding. You can know what the facts and averages are, but not really understand what is going on in a particular case, which in the end, is all that is relevant to you.

Dichotomy 22: Desire vs Freedom

Buddhism and psychoanalysis have different ways of addressing the problem of repression. Equanimity, recall, was Goenka's requirement for freedom for the individual. But freedom within the bounds of civilization also require equanimity (or abstaining from indulging in one's instinctual desires).

The second requirement for freedom, to understand the transient nature of thoughts, also has an analogy in psychology. In Cognitive psychology, for example, the individual is asked to recognize negative thought patterns ("I am unworthy") of thought, and to learn to dissociate from them.

According to Buddhism, the end of suffering is an achievable goal. But it cannot be achieved through unconditional love that could remove this sense of unworthiness, and not through striving for perfection either. Rather, the end of suffering can be achieved through the unconditional freedom of the enlightened mind.

"What, now, is the Noble Truth of the Extinction of Suffering?" asked the Buddha. "It is the complete fading away and extinction of this craving, its forsaking and abandonment, liberation and detachment from it."

The Buddha is making a radical claim – he is saying that you can isolate the sources of craving in your mind and become liberated from them and unattached to them. All you need to do is recognize the true nature of craving.

As Epstein explains in *Thoughts Without a Thinker,* the psychoanalysts tell us that instinctual drives (erotic, aggressive, narcissistic) are inborn and inescapable. It is something we must accept, whether we like it or not.

Definition of the Ego

Freud described the ego as the realistic psychological mechanism that mediates between your id (animalistic desires) and ego (moral compass).

The traditional way the individual is taught to think, is that they must cultivate a personal identity, and freely choose their goals and values. And the "ego" is colloquially referred to as pride or conceit.

By cultivating an identity, they can lead an authentic existence and participate in the social sphere in a meaningful way. Their thoughts and feelings are who they are, and they must take them seriously. This personal identity is quite stable, it rarely, if ever, changes.

The profound insight from Buddhism is to understand that your thoughts are not the same as *you*. That the things which you have worked hard to achieve, and the goals that you have adopted throughout your life, are not who you are, but a construction. Jung called this "the persona" – the social personality you have built. Freud called it the "ego."

One might object that these goals, thoughts, and desires are the story of their life, and if these do not explain who they are, then what does? What tangible, communicable alternative is there to explain a person's identity?

The answer to the first question is that they cannot be you since you were not in control of them.

You are not in control of your thoughts or feelings, since they appear automatically, involuntarily – seemingly out of thin air, and often, contrary to your desire. Since *you* have no control of them, how can they be *you*? Thoughts are useful, and central to survival, but once they are taken too seriously, and the individual cannot turn them off, then life becomes nothing but a never-ending reaction to arbitrary thoughts and feelings.

Either these thoughts induce happiness, sadness, regret, or pride, or they provoke action or rumination. The individual goes through life treating their thoughts as a fundamental part of who they are, the conscious "I" who has dreams, visions, concerns, relationships, and a personal narrative. But the error in doing so is not recognizing that thoughts take a life of their own, they desire to continue thinking about other thoughts.

The primary function of thoughts is more thinking.

As for values and goals. They, like thoughts, are beyond your control. If they were not biologically programmed into you in some way, then you were heavily influenced by your environment, role models, and circumstances. So, even if you assume that you have voluntarily shaped part of your identity, out of your own free will, then it is a negligible part, and not one worth identifying with too strongly.

As for the alternative to the ego, as it is traditionally known – this will be the subject of other chapters in this book. In short, the Freudian answer is "nothing" – you are Self-conflicted individual, because you have various impulses that are war with each other. The best that you can hope for is to find a reasonable compromise between these sub-personalities (id, ego, superego), so that you can live a minimally psychologically turbulent life.

Jung, his rebellious student, offered a different answer. The real "you" does exist, it is deep within you, and it is the Self. It is the part of you that is constant throughout time. Individuation, the natural state of the development of the individual's psyche, is a process by which you get closer to the Self. And there are ways to expedite this process and ways to slow it down. The opposite of the "Self" is the false ego (or the persona) – the mask you wear in public or at work.

Girard, whose ideas I will discuss at the end of the book, offers a different answer altogether. He says that the true "Self" is the other. Here, we have the ultimate dichotomy of the Self, between the individual and their double. Girard's idea is that he had discovered, by reading all the greatest works of literature, a common theme that yielded insight into the true nature of human desire. Essentially, all our desires, other than those related to food and shelter, are borrowed from others. According to Girard's Mimetic Theory, we have no idea what is worth desiring, so we desire the desires of another person, who is someone that we view as superior to ourselves (a model).

I will go into each of these ideas into much more detail in the rest of the book, but for now, notice that all of them essentially agree with the Eastern idea that our thoughts, values, and goals are not as solid or authentic as we would like to think.

Freud's conception of the Self is rooted in biology, particularly Darwinian evolution, so the Self is nothing but primal urges (id) in conflict with more advanced cognitive faculties (ego and superego). Freud concluded that the Self is divided against itself, and since it is divided, then the whole idea of having a coherent, consistent Self is illusory.

Jung's concept of the deeper Self, which is yet to be realized, inaccessible to our conscious minds, and can only unfold through a lengthy process also suggest that he rejected the traditional concept of the egoic Self.

Girard, with his theory of mimetic desire, clearly does not think that the individual has any authentic desires, and thus the notion of identifying fully with one's desires as if they are them, would be a ludicrous idea.

The Eastern teaching, which is to absolve the ego, was never challenged by psychoanalysts, philosophers, and in some cases, scientists in the west. If anything, this idea was extensively corroborated by various people over time, each coming to the same conclusion in a different way.

One vocal proponent of the Eastern school in the West was Alan Watts, a British writer who became famous for popularizing ideas from Buddhism, Taoism, and Hinduism in the 1960's. He argued that Buddhism can be a form of psychotherapy. And sure enough, a few decades later, plenty of books (*Buddhist Psychology and Cognitive-Behavioral Therapy: A Clinician's Guide*, *Psychotherapy and Buddhism: Toward an Integration*, *Altered Traits: Science Reveals How Meditation Changes Your Mind, Brain, and Body*, *Why Buddhism is True*, *Waking Up*, *Thoughts without a Thinker*) have emerged that do explore the link between Buddhism and psychotherapy or other forms of therapy such as CBT (Cognitive Behavioral Therapy).

Not to mention the many parallels can be drawn between Eastern religious thought and psychotherapy – including developing a distant relationship from the thinking Self, the acknowledgement of the unconscious (although early Buddhist scholars did not explicitly call it that), and the lack of total identification with the egoic Self.

Watts often commented on thinkers like Jung. But Jung, for example, warned against getting caught up in the Eastern way of thinking. The danger for the individual in the West, according to Jung, was losing their own ancestral identity.

It was better to integrate the archetypal ideas of Western civilization into one's consciousness, than seek answers from the East.

Jung believed this because he thought that a collective unconscious existed, that was passed down across the generations, and it was far more likely for the individual in the West to respond the symbols that existed in the lives of their ancestors rather than get acclimated into a foreign culture, where one has no lineage.

And yet, Jung's brand of psychology is markedly Eastern. While it may have deeper roots in Gnosticism and a heavy influence from Romanticism, there is no question that many Taoist and Buddhist concepts have analogies in Jung's work. Essentially, Jung argued against one-sidedness – being too invested in any extreme. The danger in being extremely invested in one point of view, is in ignoring one's shadow side and thus being a victim of unconscious forces. Since the psyche innately and constantly seeks equilibrium, any conscious choice towards one end of the extreme will move the psyche (in the continental sense) out of a state of balance, which is why there will be an inevitable unconscious restoration of this balance - the individual will be driven to act in ways that are contradictory to what they express or identify with consciously.

The person who is too invested in doing good, and ignores their evil shadow, will become a victim of their shadow – they will behave in ways that contradict their conscious intentions. If a person is an adamant, no nonsense rationalist, then they are at risk of being overtaken by a current of irrationality. If a person says that they are motivated by love and kindness, then hatred and spitefulness will influence their unconscious actions.

Five Aggregates

When he taught his students, the Buddha divided experience into five aggregates.

1. eyes and ears
2. basic feelings;
3. perceptions (of, say, identifiable sights or sounds)
4. "mental formations" (a big category that includes complex emotions, thoughts, inclinations, habits, decisions)
5. "consciousness," or awareness—notably, awareness of the contents of the other four aggregates.

The Buddha went through this list and asked if any of these five aggregates can be considered the Self. He then concluded, that since you have no control over any of them, therefore, you cannot say that they are part of the Self. You cannot control the existence of a particular feeling, physical organ, awareness, thoughts, or emotions, and therefore, how can you say that any of these are a part of the Self?

*The Buddha's discourse on
engagement suggests an
appealingly simple model:
liberation consists of changing
the relationship between your
consciousness and the things
you normally think of as its
"contents"— your feelings, your
thoughts, and so on. Once you
realize that these things are "not
Self," the relationship of your
consciousness to them
becomes more like
contemplation than
engagement, and your
consciousness is liberated. And
the "you" that remains—the you
that, in that first discourse on
the not-Self, the Buddha depicts
as liberated—is this liberated
consciousness.*

Why Buddhism is True, Wright

So, if we follow this line of thought, the
observing Self is the liberated Self. If I become
aware of my thoughts, it is the part of my
consciousness that is aware of my thoughts that
is the true Self. And the ruminations and
automatic thoughts that are being examined, are
simply by-products of an illusory ego that has

been constructed, and because they are involuntary, they cannot be the real "I".

The conclusion, the reconciliation between both right-brained and left-brained perspectives, is that there is a false "I", and that is what we call the ego, the personal narrative, and the culmination of thoughts, feelings, and relationships. While it is false, it is nonetheless real and important. There is a "true I" which is my conscious awareness, the experiencer who exists in the present, who does not have pretention or baggage, and who is in control. The objective ought to be, to be careful from too closely identifying with the "false I" and to develop a stronger "true I". The reason you want to do this is because the "true I" is more attuned to the present, and not a victim to useless, repetitive ruminations. The "false I" is an unconscious victim to arbitrary forces that one has no control over. The compromise between these two selves is a fact that constantly needs to be negotiated.

The Illusion of Separateness

The biggest taboo of all is knowing who we really are behind the mask of our Self as presented to the world. Through our focus on ourselves and the

Watts was very explicit in his affinity with the Eastern traditions. He believed that in the West, the individual is forced to narrow their consciousness rather than expand it. That through the various social roles one takes, the individual becomes further estranged from herself.

To understand what Watts is saying, we need to revisit Freud, who posited that infants have a primary narcissism – a claim that was later disputed by Melanie Klein and others. Basically, Freud thought that it was only later in life that people develop secondary narcissism.

What is primary narcissism? And what is secondary narcissism?

Primary narcissism is the lack of differentiation between the Self and the world. The infant, for example, cannot see the boundary that separates them from the external world. Secondary narcissism is what the individual develops as an adult. When they do not invest their libidinal energies on external objects, then they fall back on themselves, they become preoccupied with the "I."

According to Watts, reality is the stage we occupy as infants, and the illusion is what we acquire as adults – the illusion of separateness. In other words, Watts thinks that the individual, like the child, should feel like they are connected to everything else, and fail to separate between the boundaries of their ego and the external world. He thought that the adult develops a separate ego and develops the belief that they are separate from everything else – that is when things go awry. And secondary narcissism, or the ego falling in love with itself, is just a symptom of this pathology.

Watts noted that Freud was influenced by "reductionism" – the nineteenth century fashion that felt the need to put down all human intelligence and culture by calling it an arbitrary by-product of blind forces. Yet people have hypnotized themselves into believing in the hoax of egocentricity.

Thus, we are told that we have authentic, separate individualities, and yet, we are mere by products of blind forces.

This ego-fiction is not essential to the individual. Each person is a branch of the tree of humanity, but differentiation does not mean separation. The apple may be different from the branch it hangs from, but the apple and the tree are clearly connected. This is like McGilchrist's delineation between distinction and separation.

Man is conditioned to believe in this ego fiction, which creates in him a sense of alienation from everything else. He feels as though there is him, his thoughts, desires, and feelings, and then there is the rest of the world, as something that is totally different.

This implants in him the desire to get one up on nature, to conquer it and to defeat everything that is separate from his individual body. But, of course, this is absurd.

The individual works for a vision that will never be fulfilled. He works for the promise of tomorrow, a future in which the impossible will happen. So, he lives always in the future, incapable of living in the present.

Watts and other thinkers who have been influenced by Eastern philosophy like Tolle and Jung, consistently make these criticisms about the Westernized, scientific-minded man. The critique is always the same - that the modern Western mind believes that it is separate from nature, that it thinks that it ought to dominate and control nature, "playing God" so to speak. And that one must constantly work towards a shaping the future.

At one point, "playing God" seemed like a futile thing to do. But the idea has become less ridiculous with time. Watts could not have foreseen which technologies would emerge half a century after his death. If he were alive today, he could not say that "playing God" was futile or impossible, but that it was unwise.

Watts was highly critical of formal education, an education that consists of a series of steps, where each step prepares you for the next great moment, until finally, you get into university. And if you are very clever, you manage to stay on indefinitely by going to graduate school and becoming a permanent student.

Otherwise, you join the outside world of family-raising, business, and profession. But even at work, each stage is another step, which promises to carry you towards a great moment. But by the time you get there, to the final point, towards retirement, to enjoy the fruits of your labor, your life of anxiety and emotions have left you with a "weak heart, false teeth, prostate trouble, sexual impotence, fuzzy eyesight, and a vile digestion."

Again, it's important to not go too far and understand the subtle point being made. Watts was not saying that responsibility was bad, but there was such a thing as being a little too responsible. Because formal education and modern industrial society instills in us an orientation towards planning and accomplishing, we are robbed of the simple pleasures of life which can only be experienced by living in the present. We have substituted an error free life, for a life worth living.

Technology is man's way of controlling life, and in many ways, it has enhanced man's existence, providing comfort, transportation, convenience, clean drinking water, sanitation, and artificial light. Thanks to technology, we are much smarter and more comfortable. But the other side of the coin is that we have become more Self-destructive.

In the past, the recognition of life's impermanence led to withdrawal. Monks, ascetics, and hermits tried to exorcise their desires, to regard the world with benign resignation, or to try to draw back into the depths of consciousness to unite with a deeper Self. Others saw the world as a state of probation, where material goods were to be used as if they were loans from the Almighty, where the point of life was loving devotion to God and to man.

Yet both these responses are based on the initial supposition that the individual is a separate ego, thus any task undertaken on this basis including religion will be sell-defeating. Just because it is a hoax from the beginning, the personal ego can make only a phony response to life. For the world is an ever elusive and ever-disappointing mirage only from the standpoint of someone standing aside from it as if it were quite other than himself and then trying to grasp it.

Alan Watts, The Book: On the Taboo Against Knowing Who You Are

Watts is saying that these ascetic solutions are illusory as well because they start from the presupposition that an "I" exists in the first place. Once you recognize that there is no "I", then there is nothing to be disappointed about.

Thus, he offers a third response, which we are conditioned to ignore. It is not withdrawal, but the fullest collaboration with the world, and knowing that the only real "I" is the endless process. Our bodies and senses know this, but our thin ray of conscious attention has been taught so well to ignore it. That is why we are genuine fakes and why the conservative psychoanalyst, Carl Jung, got it right when he opted to preserve tradition in some way, and offered his patients a more fulfilling answer that connected them with their ancestry.

Instead of thinking of the Self as fragmented, the Self was, in fact, connected deeply with the past. And archetypal symbols that exist in the unconscious of each person are proof of this continuous identity, according to Jung.

But there seems to be an irreconcilable problem with the analysis Watts gives here, and the point that Tolle made earlier, is that it commits the same error as Freud, unwittingly. Freud's reductionism may have led him to believe that the Self was disconnected and fragmented, which led him to assume that a Self that is free from the past was freer than one that was not, but Watts' idea leads him to believe the opposite absurdity – that the Self is not in important ways disconnected from everything else.

As I have mentioned before, while there may be a lost sense of connectedness, there is undeniably a sense of separateness. It may be that the individual changes and metamorphosizes, but change is not indicative of an illusion, neither is lack of control. I may be partially in control of my thoughts, and not the same person I once was, but that doesn't mean that there is no sense of continuity whatsoever, that there is no 'ego'. And in any case, if there is no ego at all, then who is doing the thinking, and for who's benefit? Who is the person asking all these questions? If the ego is boundless, then why are these ideas only accessible to my conscious awareness and can only be made available to others if I consciously express them?

When I use the left-brain way of thinking, these notions quickly run into trouble. They are Self-contradictory and nonsensical. If I wanted to apply right-brained thinking, I would say that my left-brain is missing the point. It is not that I don't have a sense that I am different, or that my thoughts are my own, or that there is an "I", but that these are simply illusions. Consider the fact that if I try to observe my thoughts, a peculiar thing happens. I am observing the thoughts of my "Self", but then who is the "I"?

The Buddhistic answer is that the Self that is doing the automatic thinking is not the "I" but is unconscious.

One interesting experiment you can try on yourSelf, is to watch, like a hawk, for your next thought. Close your eyes and pay very close attention to the next thought you are going to have.

What you will notice, if you do this exercise, is that it will take a long time for the next thought to appear. If you are not in this vigilant state of awareness, your thoughts tend to wander. Some monks practice the tradition of creeping up behind each other when one of them is meditating and hitting them with a stick. A person whose mind is not wandering, and is fully alert, can sense movement behind them and move.

Mindfulness: A Deceptive Cure

In recent years, there has been an acceptance in the West of the benefits of Eastern practices that used to be considered esoteric (yoga, meditation).

In *Altered Traits*, a book by Daniel Goleman and Richard Davidson, we are told about the failure of clinical psychology in trying to cure the problems of the mind. A comparison is made between the Western and Eastern approach.

In the West, clinical psychology tries to fix a specific problem like high anxiety by focusing on that one thing, while Asian psychologies have a wider lens and offer ways to enhance our positive side. Notice that this is akin to the dichotomy posited by Ian McGilchrist in *The Master and His Emissary.*

Richard, one of the authors of *Altered Traits*, became interested in consciousness after reading the works of Aldous Huxley, R.D Laing, Martin Buber, and Ram Dass. But these interests were driven underground during his college years in New York University, where professors were staunch behaviorists (followers of B. F. Skinner). They thought that observable behavior was the only way of understanding the mind, while looking inside the mind was a taboo waste of time. They believed that mental life was irrelevant to understanding behavior.

When French poet and Nobel laureate Romain Rolland became a disciple of the Indian saint Sri Ramakrishna near the beginning of the 20th century, he wrote to Freud about the mystical state he experienced. Freud diagnosed it as regression to infancy.

In the 1960's, psychologists dismissed drug-triggered altered states as artificially induced psychosis. And yet, as described in *Altered Traits*, there are tangible, scientifically measurable benefits to meditation.

So, who is right?

There are indeed benefits from meditation, but not for everyone. Dr. Farias, in this article, says:

....in my new study, which reviews over 40 years of the science of meditation and mindfulness-based therapies, suggests that these practices can also lead to negative effects in about 8 per cent of individuals — from increases in anxiety, depression and stress, to unusual experiences like hallucinations.

Concerns about meditation were irrational in the 1960's, we are told in *Altered States.* But were these reservations unfounded?

As early as 1976, Arnold Lazarus, one of the forefathers of cognitive behavioral therapy, raised concerns about transcendental meditation, the mantra-based practice then in vogue. "When used indiscriminately," he warned, "the procedure can precipitate serious psychiatric problems such as depression, agitation, and even schizophrenic decompensation." Lazarus had by then treated several "agitated, restive" patients whose symptoms seemed to worsen after meditating. He came to believe that the

practice, while beneficial for
many, was likely harmful to
some.

Meditation, contrary to how it is marketed, is not for relaxation and it is not a convenient way to gain health benefits. It is an ancient practice pursued by those who have committed themselves to a spiritual life.

The Buddhist ascetics who took up meditation in the fifth century BC did not view it as a form of stress relief. "These contemplative practices were invented for monastics who had renounced possessions, social position, wealth, family, comfort, and work," writes David McMahan, a professor of religious studies at Franklin and Marshall College, in a 2017 book, *Meditation, Buddhism, and Science*. Monks and nuns sought to transcend the world and its cycles of rebirth and awaken in nirvana, an unfathomable state of equanimity beyond space and time, or at least avoid being reincarnated as a mountain goat or a hungry spirit in the hell realm underground.

As Mark Epstein said *in Thoughts Without a Thinker*, for the Western mind, the idea of Buddhism alone is too strange, because the westerner has a different starting point from the easterner.

The easterner feels like he belongs to a tight network, and meditation is a way for him to estrange himself temporarily, so that he may experience his own individuality. But the person in the West does not have this problem. Instead, the latter's problem is more related to enduring feelings of estrangement, and their sense of loneliness and abandonment.

Psychology has become a leading authority to answering questions that are spiritual or philosophical in nature, not because the therapist has branded themselves as the provider of spiritual solutions, but because modern society, with its increasing identification as an essentially secular, commercial, scientific civilization that is the proud product of the Enlightenment, sways the individual towards seeking spiritual cures, not from shamans or men in religious garment, but from therapists (men of "science").

Zen

Zen says concepts are illusions and that the Ego is an illusion.

Psychology has proven to be an effective tool when wielded in the right circumstances. The only thing that has truly been proven is that a universal software has not been discovered. But the response should not be to do away with psychology altogether merely because it has not given us concrete answers to our deepest questions.

I have referred to powerful critiques of psychology, not to dismiss it, but to highlight an important point. Despite a century and half of trying to understand the human mind, and countless technological inventions used to study the brain, we are still not much closer to solving the mysteries that the ancient Greeks pondered about. We still don't understand how physical reality can give rise to consciousness, where our desires originated, why we are torn between various dichotomies, why we have an innate need to worship, and to congregate in group rituals, and why certain ideas have such a powerful influence on our lives (even without our conscious awareness).

That is not to say that we have not gained insight. We have. But there are no simple solutions to man's predicaments. The risk of turning inwards, as the discussion on narcissism and mindfulness suggests, is that the individual that is too preoccupied with how they feel risks alienating themselves from reality and from others.

As Burton showed in her book, the desire to get rid of religion has only propagated new forms of religion, far less rational and coherent. Even the attempt to turn to the East and embrace introspective techniques like meditation is fraught with problems that most media channels never discuss.

In short, despite the progress we have made, we are still mostly clueless about the inner workings of the human mind. If we think about the crazed German philologist who warned that science was inimical to life, we may offer up a cheeky smirk. But then when we consider the threat of nuclear warfare, biological warfare, and the threat of A.I in the future, suddenly, and yet again, Nietzsche emerges more as a prophetic figure than a lunatic.

Conclusion

The Manipulation of the Self

It is now time to review. In the beginning, I discussed man's basic predicament – to exist as disconnected from himself, living beings, and nature, yet to be asked to sacrifice himself for the greater good.

We went through a brief tour of the fundamental psychoanalytic ideas of the 20th century. We explored the various conflicts that exist within the psyche of the individual, and we learned that man is also disconnected from himself, or put another way, the different parts of his psyche are disconnected from each other, and always in conflict. The essential disconnection is one that concerns the ego. In the great debate about human nature, we have seen two sides, one that confirms the reality of the ego, the importance of the ego fictions that we construct for ourselves, and another side that denies the existence of the ego, calling it an illusion.

Recall that in the introduction, I mentioned the difference between western and eastern thought. This distinction is again relevant here. Buddha argued that we construct ego fictions. Jung, who was also influenced by eastern philosophy, agreed – he acknowledged that the persona was a fake mask, and that the ego was not one's true identity, it was separate from man's authentic Self. Schopenhauer argued that the solution to man's predicament was the denial of the will, thus the denial of one's own ego. I am not saying that these thoughts are identical, they are not. But they do make a similar underlying point about the illusion of the human ego.

On the other side of the debate, we have Nietzsche, who disagreed, he advanced the concept of the superman, and argued that there was hope for the individual ego, indeed, that we should glorify the ego's will to power rather than deny it.

As Girard noted, Marx believed that man was ruled by economic drives while Freud thought that man was ruled by Eros and Thanatos. Both thought that man was less autonomous than he believed, in other words, they were ruled by desires outside of themselves. And yet unlike Nietzsche, they tried to reconcile this conflict. Marx sought to redistribute wealth, while Freud tried to rid man of guilt, to relax the punitive force of the superego. But Nietzsche wanted to give full reign to man's instinct, despite knowing that it would lead to conflict.

P.F Skinner, the behaviorist, believed that man's internal life was not important, all that mattered was stimulus and response. In that sense, Skinner was quite close to Eastern thought, since he accepted that the ego was a fiction, and believed that it was external factors that shape the individual, rather conscious determination.

Girard noticed what the psychoanalysts of the 20th century all failed to notice. Or, if they did notice, they did not adequately emphasize it, and it was the role of mimesis in the creation of human desire. Mimesis is the ultimate dagger to the ego fiction. If our non-instinctual desires are replicas of one another, and not determined by our authentic will, then what purpose is there to hold on to our ego fictions?

The major thinkers throughout history can all agree on one thing, and it is that external entities (mimesis, primordial drives, economic incentives) that drive the behavior of people, and not Self-determination. Ellul and Kurzweil, although opposites in every single way, would agree with this idea and would say that technology is like a primordial force that seeks to totalize nature, and the human being can only be an instrument in this process, and not a determining agent.

Popular culture gives a lot of weight to individual choice. Most people live their lives truly believing in the reality of their egos. They think that the choices they make are their own, that their desires are authentic, and that their motivations, tastes, and aversions are unique. But deep introspection has always led the introspective man to conclude that it is a mistake to take the ego so seriously.

Before the philosophers and the psychologists, most religious traditions recognized the danger of over-identifying with one's ego fiction. A few, like Nietzsche, celebrated it despite understanding its folly, but most thinkers recognized the illusory nature of the ego and tried to reconcile it.

By identifying with the ego, man disconnects from either himself, others, and nature. He creates boundaries where none exist. And since he cannot but identify as a Self, whether this Self is an illusion does not matter, since he feels that he is distinct form others, then he finds himself in a disconnected and alienated state. Man's primal instincts, as Freud noted, are denied by the forces of civilization. So, how does the individual reconcile this disconnection?

One answer offered is sublimation – to put one's energies into the production of socially useful works, while individuation (the Jungian answer) was offered as a cure for man's loss of differentiation and autonomy. Girard's Mimetic Theory, on the other hand, explains the fundamental danger of choosing the wrong models for imitation (either because they are internal models or because they motivated by lowly ideals).

The appropriate thing to do is not to avoid mimesis, that would be like avoiding being human, but to try to find more positive models. In trying to do so, it would be helpful to place less emphasis on differentiation, and more emphasis on the truth - even if it leads to dangerous realizations about the true nature of human beings.

We also learned that learned that therapy is primarily interested in the socialization of people into compliant and docile members of the group, and this may come at the expense of individuality. So, we have seen how even therapy can contribute to the further disconnectedness of man. And if this was not enough, the removal of the religious substructure by the modern secular persuasion turned the individual inwards, towards vanity and narcissism, and towards a Self-defeating therapeutic sensibility. Even meditation, which is in modern times touted as the miracle cure for all ailments, must be practiced with caution.

Therefore, our vanity and narcissism are often the result of our failure to recognize the ultimate dichotomy, the double. As Girard explained, we are never in pursuit of an object, we are in pursuit of someone else's desire of an object. We mistake this other person's desire for our own, and in fact, it must be the case that we do not notice this process.

Dichotomy 23: Separate Vs Connected

A rough way to summarize the binary nature of human beings would be to think of the individual as a creature who is constantly at odds with himself, always torn between two conflicting ideals or modes of being. If we wanted to really simplify these ideas to their very essence, then we can say that the individual is confronted with an eternal metaphysical dilemma, between being connected and separated – from himself, others, and nature itself. The idea of connectedness and separateness can be related to the left brain – right brain dichotomy. Of course, separateness would refer to the left brain while connectedness would refer to the right.

With all these dichotomies and schisms, there is plenty of confusion. That may explain why so many have turned inwards, towards themselves. In Girardian language, the models are no longer clear. Who is the spiritual model for the western or Eastern individual? Is it the priest or the guru? Is it the trans-humanist in Silicon Valley? Is it Neil deGrasse Tyson from Cosmos or Stephen Hawking? Is it Elon musk or Oprah?

The internet and the connectedness of the world has punched a hole through the subject-model paradigm. No longer does the individual grow up knowing who ought to be admired and who ought to be scorned, based on a simple passing down of tradition. The modern individual is given the task, if he dares to engage in it, in figuring it out for themselves. That is, in choosing their own model from a selection of hundreds, or thousands.

But in the end, you have the freedom to live in a complete state of dissociation, where you exist as pure awareness. Your thoughts may come and go, you may feel despair and excitement, but they are just like the wind, they are nothing to be taken seriously, nothing to commit to. The only experience you take seriously is your direct experience of reality. That is the only thing that is real. There are no models whose desires you care about or want to emulate.

On the other hand, you can go in the totally opposite direction, and you can become wholly identified with your ego. You can create a personal narrative, set several arbitrary goals, work incessantly towards them, achieve milestones, fulfill your dreams, try to experience as much pleasure as possible (while accepting the cost that comes in the form of corresponding pain), and live a full life of ups and downs, elation and depression, victories, and defeats.

And of course, there is a third option. And it is to occupy a point of tension in between both extremes. This is a very tricky path. It is far more difficult than the first two. Your brain does not like contradiction or cognitive dissonance. It is unlikely that you have come to appreciate the wisdom of contradiction. So, choosing this path will force you to come across many internal conflicts, in addition to the external conflicts which you will face. In addition to solving real life problems, you will need to constantly decide to what extent you want to devote your life to the ego and to what extent you want to devote your life to no-ego.

You may wonder how I consider the ego driven life a serious choice after I have just said that it is a fiction. Let me explain, Fictions have a bad reputation. Harari, for example, uses the word fictions in a somewhat derogatory way. But these "fictions" are not really fictions. That is, they don't refer to complete fantasy. Some fictions are better described as narratives, which we may be more or less true, but essential for life.

As Fingarette delightfully argues in his short book, Self-deception, to deceive oneself is an inescapable fact of life. If you didn't do so, you would not be able to watch a movie (make believe), you would not be able to ignore noises in a coffee shop and spontaneously pay attention when you hear a familiar voice. Without Fictions, societies would cease to function. So, before you get upset that your ego is a fiction, notice that everything that exists is a fiction and some are much more grounded in reality than others.

Works Cited

Bon, G. L. (1895). *The Crowd: A Study of the Popular Mind* .

Bostrom, N. (2014). *Superintelligence: Paths, Dangers, Strategies.* Oxford University Press.

Burton, T. I. (2020). *Strange Rites: New Religions for a Godless World.* PublicAffairs.

Ellenberger, H. F. (1970). *The Discovery of the Unconscious: The History and Evolution of Dynamic Psychiatry.* Basic Books.

Foucault, M. (1961). *Madness and Civilization: A History of Insanity in the Age of Reason.* Vintage .

Freud, S. (1920). *Beyond the Pleasure Principle .* W.W. Norton & Company .

Freud, S. (1930). *Civilization and its Discontents .* W. W. Norton Company.

Fromm, E. (1973). *The Anatomy of Human Destructiveness .* Open Road Media.

Garrels, S. R. (2011). *Mimesis and Science: Empirical Research on Imitation and the Mimetic Theory of Culture and Religion.* Michigan State University Press.

Girard, R. (1978). *Things Hidden Since the Foundation of the World.* Stanford University Press .

Goleman, D., & Davidson, R. J. (2017). *Altered Traits: Science Reveals How Meditation Changes Your Mind, Brain, and Body.* Avery Publishing Group.

Hobbes, T. (1651). *Leviathan.* Penguin Books.

Jung, C. (1952). *Answer to Job.* Princeton University Press.

Jung, C. (1959). *The Archetypes and the Collective Unconscious.* Princeton University Press (NJ).

Jung, C. (1961). *The Undiscovered Self.* Signet .

Lasch, C. (1978). *The Culture of Narcissism: American Life in An Age of Diminishing Expectations.* W. W. Norton Company .

McGilchrist, I. (2009). *The Master and His Emissary: The Divided Brain and the Making of the Western World.* Yale University Press.

Meier, C. A. (1977). *Personality: The Individuation Process in the Light of C.G. Jung's Typology.* Daimon Verlag.

Michel Foucault, R. H. (1961). *Madness and Civilization: A History of Insanity in the Age of Reason.* Vintage .

Nietzsche, F. (1871). *The Birth of Tragedy.* Penguin Classics.

Nietzsche, F. (1882). *The Gay Science.* Random House.

Nietzsche, F. (1887). *On The Genealogy of Morals .* Vintage Books.

Nietzsche, F. (1889). *Richard Wagner in Bayreuth.* Dodo Press .

Palaver, W. (2008). *René Girard's Mimetic Theory.* Michigan State University Press.

Rieff, P. (2007). *The Triumph of the Therapeutic .* Intercollegiate Studies Institute.

Szasz, T. (1961). *The Myth of Mental Illness: Foundations of a Theory of Personal Conduct.* Harper .

Tarde, G. (1903). *The Laws of Imitation.* Henry Holt and Company.

Tolle, E. (1997). *The Power of Now: A Guide to Spiritual Enlightenment.* New World Library.

Watts, A. W. (1966). *The Book on the Taboo Against Knowing Who You Are.* Vintage .

Wright, R. (2017). *Why Buddhism is True: The Science and Philosophy of Meditation and Enlightenment.* Simon Schuster.

1
https://en.wikipedia.org/wiki/Hard_problem_of_consciousn
ess

i https://pubmed.ncbi.nlm.nih.gov/23834638/)

ii
https://www.theatlantic.com/science/archive/2015/08/psychology-studies-reliability-reproducability-nosek/402466/

-

iii Faridah Djellal, Faïz Gallouj. The laws of imitation and invention: Gabriel Tarde and the evolutionary economics of innovation. 2014